Find Your Self in the Bible

Find Your Self in the Bible

A Guide to Relational Bible Study

for Small Groups

Karl A. Olsson

AUGSBURG PUBLISHING HOUSE
MINNEAPOLIS, MINNESOTA

To my mother
who, by not overselling the Bible,
freed me up to love it.

FIND YOUR SELF IN THE BIBLE

Copyright © 1974 Augsburg Publishing House

Library of Congress Catalog Card No. 73-88605

International Standard Book No. 0-8066-1408-0

Manufactured in the United States of America

CONTENTS

Introduction 7

1. My Five Ways of Looking at the Bible 11
   GROUP DESIGN 1 31

2. The Kingdom of Right Relationships 33
   GROUP DESIGN 2 44

3. The Risk of Relationships 45
   GROUP DESIGN 3 56

4. How Can God Use My Game Plan? 59
   GROUP DESIGN 4 68

5. Am I a Mask or a Face? 69
   GROUP DESIGN 5 78

6. A Plane Made to Fly 79
   GROUP DESIGN 6 85

7. Much Wine and Little 87
   GROUP DESIGN 7 91

8. Oil of Gladness 93
   GROUP DESIGN 8 101

Creating Your Own Relational Bible Studies 103

Guidelines for Ten Relational Bible Studies 105

INTRODUCTION

This is a "how to" book. It is, however, not designed to teach people how to read the Bible with understanding, how to use it in teaching or evangelism, how to quote from it, or how to reinterpret it for contemporary minds. All these objectives are proper, and I have no quarrel with them. But they are not mine.

This book tries to suggest ways of making the Bible personal and relational. Many of us have been trained to look at the Bible as the "good book," that is, full of good messages or maxims or instructive stories or as a map for our pilgrimage to the Celestial City. In other words, a store of general truths. But we have not been taught with equal diligence that the Bible is a *real* book, real for me. Which means concrete and particular, focused on my *now*.

Find Your Self in the Bible tries to present biblical materials in such a way that they achieve a personal focus. This is done by having the author "model" the biblical passage by experiences from his own life. Such experiences are not presented because they are extraordinary, but because they may help the reader to identify with them and through them with the biblical passage.

7

Chapters 1-2 present my personal introduction to the Bible as well as the "philosophy of relationships" which informs the book. Chapters 3-8 are relational Bible studies of the type described above.

After each of the chapters I have included a group design which can be used to give personal focus to the topic being considered. These designs may be used at the conclusion of a Bible study in which the materials have been presented. The process would be this:

1. The leader of the meeting uses the Bible passage and the interpretation included in the chapter as a background for his own modeling. The effectiveness of the presentation will depend on the leader's willingness to identify with the biblical passage.

2. This presentation may be followed by a few moments of general discussion to clarify the concepts of the study or to emphasize the significant points.

3. The members of the group are then asked to get into groups of two, three, or four (as suggested in the chapter) and to proceed with the group design of the chapter under consideration.

At the conclusion of the book there are two additional resources.

The first is a suggested design for *Creating Your Own Relational Bible Studies* on the theory that it is the role of the church and the clergy to enable and equip the laity for effective witness and ministry. The more "do-it-yourself" experiences we can provide for one another the more rapidly we move from passive observation to active participation in the redemptive processes to which the church is committed.

The second resource, *Guidelines for Ten Relational Bible Studies,* offers brief outlines that can be developed into group designs.

The book is designed also for individual study. The various group designs may be used effectively as personal inventories or as "starters" for informal in-depth conversations.

I am grateful to the Faith at Work staff for reading the manuscript and for making many valuable suggestions; to Bruce Larson and Keith Miller for reading and evaluating it; to Lyman Coleman for stimulating my interest in this approach to the Bible; and to my family for a loving uncritical reading. A special word of thanks to Paula Breen for typing the manuscript and enabling the process of making it into a book.

1

MY FIVE WAYS
OF LOOKING
AT THE BIBLE

This is to be a series of what I have chosen to call "Relational Bible Studies—by which I mean, studies designed to give the Bible a personal focus.

Looking back on my experience of the Scriptures, I confess to an ambivalence. I have been alternately attracted to and repelled by the Bible. This doubleness was with me at the very beginning, and it has remained until quite recently.

I believe that the reasons for my negative feelings about the Scriptures are personal; that is, they emerged from the way in which people communicated the Bible to me. But the same can certainly be said about my earliest positive feelings.

Some of the people who surrounded me in my childhood said that they loved the Bible, but they had a way of talking about it which turned me off. From many of them the Scriptures came through as a resounding "No" or a "no—no". Or, worse yet, as an undramatic staple, as, for example oatmeal—simple, nourishing, and bleak.

I do not recall that many of these people used the Bible to affirm creation as a gift or to emphasize the meaning of love between human beings. The new heaven and the new earth were identified with a kingdom beyond time, and the love which was stressed was either entirely vertical (God's undeserved love for me) or obligatory. When we children fought, the community enjoined us to love one another. But love between people as a way of life and as a present joy seems to have been feared as something too close to sensual love. Human love was implied but not easily expressed.

There were notable exceptions, and among them I must mention my own family and certain teachers both in the public school and in the Sunday school. My father, whose love for the Bible was almost inordinate, contributed to my positive feeling for the book. Although I may often have wished for more festival in him, he had a compensating virtue. He was an engineer and realist and did not plunge me into the apocalyptic vortices which were fairly common in our type of dissent. And in both his words and deeds he interpreted the meaning of love in a dry way that made sense.

In this connection I recall a particularly tense time in my childhood. The end of the world had been predicted for February 6, 1925. I had already lived through an abortive crisis in 1919, but still feared the worst. I remember walking into my father's room (in the company of an older sister) late in the evening of February 5 and telling my father that I was scared. He was busy at his desk but paused long enough to say, "If you read the New Testament carefully, you will find that no one knows the day or the hour of the Lord's appearing. Tomorrow will be a day like any other day. Now go to bed and go to sleep." The dry exegesis was most comforting; we lived through the next day in equilibrium.

My mother was much more the romantic and mystic. She wove together nature and supernature. Whereas my father was always posing rabbinical questions which sought to elucidate either ethical problems or doctrinal points, my mother devoted herself to the adoration of the creation and the Creator. She did this by singing both nature lyrics and heaven hymns (I recall her full-bodied and clear soprano in the summer nights of my childhood interpreting Grieg's *"Den store vide flok"* or a slight apostrophe to a forest flower).

I believe that it was my father's biblical common sense and my mother's love of nature which made both faith and love credible. In my parents' company the Bible was manageable.

I now perceive that there were roughly five stages in my understanding and appreciation of the Scriptures, with every stage present in what followed. I see them as *Mystery, Heroics, Ethics, Theology,* and *Miracle.*

The Bible as Mystery

To begin with the Bible was just *holy.* This meant lifted up and apart. If I had known the word, I would have called it *transcendent.* It was different from the ordinary world of barking dogs, bare feet, and meat and potatoes. I could not have been more than three when I had my first remembered dream. It was a dream of a king seated on a throne, and he was splendid in scarlet and gold. I can still evoke the mood of strength and glory which the dream suggested to me. The Bible was like that.

It was a large book bound in black leather and stamped with gold lettering; it lay on a lectern in Holy Church and was read from by holy men in robes, whose voices thundered under the arches. I am sure this image of mystery was reinforced by my experience as a three-year-old of the Russian Orthodox service in Perm. At the time we attended the services, the priests wore green vestments. I remember their long hair and beards and their chanting and making the sign of the cross.

The Bible was equally black, but smaller, when it was held in the hands of earnest young men who served our mission society as lay evangelists and who sometimes concealed their shyness and their panic by shouting and weeping in the chapel. But it was no less a mystery.

For us children the Bible was a *sad* mystery. It made us silent. It was linked for us at the feeling level with the end of everything in this world: death, the churchyard, heaven. I was five when I first *felt* the churchyard. The sky was blue with white clouds, and the chestnut trees above the tombstones were spongy green. There were dark spots of shadow under the trees. A gate stood open, and the gravel walks drew us into "the resting room of the dead"—an adult phrase. We looked at the stones, their polished black surfaces clean and threatening like the marble foyer of a hospital. There were small graves and small stones for children. I remember a small pink celluloid doll on one of the graves. Children also died and went to heaven.

What was a grave? A bed or a gate to heaven? And why was it so sad even in the midst of the heaven talk? So heavy and sad? At funerals there were cakes and confections with brown and black crosses. There were coffee cakes in the shape of a cross. Was the holy always sad? The black Bible and the black hymn book with their gold crosses were like pitch-covered arks ferrying us through floods of weeping.

The Bible was also an *angry* mystery. It lay on the table in the parlor; we could leaf through it if our hands were clean. The illustrations by Doré terrified us. God seemed always hostile, hovering menacingly. There were sheets of dark water; lightning flashed, swords flamed. There was page after page of doom: the tower of Babel surrounded by raised fists and hostile faces; the towering hulk of the ark; Abraham's dagger above the boy Isaac horribly, deliciously waiting; fire and brimstone falling on the cities of the plain and people fleeing—always the flowing garments, the hurrying sandalled feet, the frightened faces; and an enraged Moses with the tablets raised like a weapon.

But the Bible was also a *joyous* mystery. Death and judgment, and even the bliss of heaven so strange and threatening, did not always vertically intrude. There were green valleys and flowering fields and there was the beautiful turbulence of biblical seas and lakes. Abraham, Jacob, Joseph, David—they did ordinary things: ate, slept, made mistakes, grumbled, tended sheep, fished, plowed fields, prayed, fell in love, grew old. And, of course, there were the festivals: Christmas with a tender light over the sheepfold and Easter with crocuses braving the chill sunlight.

I am not suggesting by this last paragraph that life is not sad and angry or that there is no room for the splendid and transcendent. What I feel in reflecting on my childhood is that meaning of a biblical kind was exclusively vertical. Holiness was unvaryingly above and beyond me; it was remote, awesome, towering. The ordinary, flat, familiar things in that universe of lightning and volcanic eruption seem not to have counted. The things I loved—forest and field and cloud and water, but more than that the minute concrete thing, the puff of dust cast up by a harrow, a bottle of buttermilk kept cool in grass, the rhythmic munching of cows, the fall of lantern light in snow, the incredible movement of a horse under me, and the play of feeling in human faces—all this had nothing to do with the Bible. Or so I seem to have been taught. The Bible said something about creation, of course, but only to rush on to the Fall and the need of a new creation. Otherwise the message was the judgment which cut like a knife blade through every act and intention, and the ultimate salvation on the other side of the sea of blood.

I now understand that the lovely horizontal things were given a special meaning by being placed in a context of divine action. I also understand that my particular kind of evangelical Protestant piety did not dare make too much of the incarnational and the coarse-grained, concrete humanity of our Lord. Even the New Testament with its smell of fish, dunged fields, fresh-cut boards, and damp sheep's wool had to hover above our life in a shimmer of unreality.

But perhaps that was the best I could ask. Those living out their lives unaware of God's life in history seem to have made even less sense of things. If anything, they loved creation less than I did. Their rootedness in time and space did not seem to permit them to celebrate the ordinary things or to bewail their transience with any greater intensity. Perhaps that was the best I could ask, but I sometimes wish that I could have allowed myself to

16

say about a scene or a relationship, "This is good." I think I would have said this without ascribing the goodness to myself. Even so, I could not say it or was not encouraged to say it.

The Bible as Heroics

The second level of biblical experience was that of *heroics*. As a young boy I was encouraged, especially by my Sunday school teachers, to find my heroes in the biblical world. I am sure that this was done with the worthiest motives. The only problem was that when you push the biblical heroes, they don't come off very well. The Bible is much too aware of the humanity of human beings to construct any useful moral fictions. Who would really want to have his child act like Jacob, Joseph, Moses, Samuel, Saul, David, or even Simon Peter? The point, of course, is that none of these people are presented as artful models of behavior at all, but as human beings who in their humanity and need reach out for God's help and blessing.

Despite this, I had well-intentioned instructors who tried to make me emulate the young David, Joseph, Daniel. If these models had been presented as human and sinful people, I may have responded, but as pious Eagle Scouts they frankly bored me. I think I felt as I did for two reasons: first, I sensed the dishonesty of making these biblical characters come off as ideals. Secondly, no biblical hero held a candle to the military titans who inhabited my interior world: Alexander, Caesar, Olav Tryggvason, Richard the Lionhearted, Gustavus Adolphus, Charles XII, George Washington, Ulysses S. Grant. In the case of the heroic secular giants, I was given no illusion of moral perfection, although their biographers sometimes tried to paste a moral on their bloody chronicles.

Here again I felt that the non-biblical greats were closer to me. They inhabited the real world. When they were hacked by a sword, they bled. When they triumphed, their victory was woven into geography and history. The biblical exploits were much more elusive. They seem to have been carried out in a territory halfway between earth and heaven. It took me a long time to understand that biblical realism (from which I was partly protected) was infinitely superior to that of secular chronicles. But when I was a child, the Bible came off second-best.

The Bible as Ethics

My next stage of biblical interpretation was the *ethical*, or perhaps more honestly, the *moralistic*. I was theoretically aware of something called grace or mercy, but compared to my schoolmates I was a combination of intellectual snobbishness, unwearying sarcasm, and frosty pietism. I did not know myself to be morally superior— for I was not—but my approach to relationships was judgmental. I came off as the critic of all sorts of slovenliness.

I was always asking the ethical questions—about drink, necking, cheating on exams, God in human experience. Of course, inside I was no different from the adolescents I studied and played with. I was a boiling caldron of lusts, greeds, ambitions, angers, fears. Secretly I envied the darker life my classmates lived openly, but outwardly I was the responsible young man—a third-rate Saul of Tarsus. And the Bible was the Law, holy and good.

By an ironic twist I embodied the very thing I had found so threatening in my childhood. I was the judge. And my support in this was the Bible. I saw myself as the biblical man. In confronting the growing humanism and paganism of the late twenties and early thirties (Nathan, Mencken, Lewis, Dreiser et al.) I cast myself in the role of the cross-bearer and Jesus-follower who was really going to make this thing work and thus confound the scoffers. I was no champion of biblical Fundamentalism, for I had abandoned the argument from authority. Rather I saw myself as a person who could incarnate the Christ ideals and accept the full measure of suffering that these entailed.

In the midst of this I met an old minister who did not struggle much with ideals but who had a compelling trust in the biblical processes of grace. He invited me to my first communion (I had been confirmed earlier), and to my protest that I was not good enough to commune he replied that worthiness was no condition for receiving the sacrament.

Taking communion did not much change my idealistic stance, but it opened a window on the complexity of human nature and prepared me for Paul's anguish in Romans 7: "I do not understand what I do; for I don't do what I would like to do, but instead I do what I hate . . . even though the desire to do good is in me, I am not able to do it" TEV.

But something else was at work within me during this time. The Bible made me an idealist, but it also pushed me in the direction of a personal mysticism. I began to believe in God's loving providence. I became convinced (and still am) that God's will is active in the people who trust him. Job's cry, "He knows the way that I take; when he has tried [tested] me, I shall come forth as gold," became one of my favorite verses. I am sure that there was both egotism and sentimentality in this belief and that I abused it fearfully. I saw myself as privileged even in the thornier circumstances of my life, and this may have prevented me from identifying with all the other rams caught in the thicket. But, on the whole, the conviction that God loved me in the midst of both my arrogance and lust and that he was designing something with me and for me—this remained one of the fixed stars of my pilgrimage.

I once tried to witness to this faith in a university study group which was reading Augustine's *Confessions*. I recall the contempt with which the young avant-garde professor of theology responded to my statement. "That," he snorted, (meaning my faith in God's active will in my life) "is nothing but Fundamentalism." And with that I was sent back to my seat. Fortunately I made no defense. I felt like a dumb kid bringing a dandelion to a botanist. I have since realized that being a dumb kid is okay and that there may be things about dandelions which being a botanist does not help you understand.

Having witnessed to this mystical-personal faith in guidance as it is revealed in the Bible, I want to state some reservations. I do not pretend to understand the will of God or to be able to systematize it. It does not make sense in any simple way. For example, some weeks ago two of my friends were killed in a private plane crash; at almost the same time another friend also crashed his small plane but was miraculously rescued. How can you be glib about that? All I can do is to weep with those who weep and rejoice with those who rejoice and to confess with Job, "Therefore I have uttered what I did not understand, things too wonderful for me, which I did not know."

The Bible as Theology

I moved next into what might be called the professional study of the Bible and the church—a study which has lasted for over three decades. In this kind of intellectual work the biblical text is an object of inquiry. Since the Bible was originally written in Hebrew and Greek, the first task of biblical scholarship is to recover the meaning of the words. This is more than finding exact equivalents. One doesn't recover the meaning of the word merely by studying a lexicon. What is required is an understanding of the particular historical circumstances which gave the words their meaning. Thus in some sense the whole ancient world must become one's oyster.

Beyond this there came the understanding and ordering of ideas which emerge in the text, what is usually called biblical theology. For a time I was interested in the social theology of the Bible; then with the coming of so-called dialectical theology I majored in the great themes of creation, judgment, and redemption. I ate, drank, and dreamt theologians like Barth, Brunner, Kierkegaard, and Reinhold Niebuhr.

During this time I was validating my faith experience by the criterion of intellectual purity. For me Barth's neo-Kantian theology with its emphasis on the unmuddied transcendence of God was, in contrast to liberal theology, a powerful word. For a time I would have no truck with anything which did not make God wholly other. I saw man crawling under a dome vaulted so far above him that all his feelings, impulses, and actions had a monumental irrelevance.

I did not then understand that I desired the same remoteness for myself. I did not have the courage or the love to struggle with the problem of involvement in my own existence. Sometimes I wanted to follow my own planetary orbit, far removed from the complex trails of other people.

But in the long run Barth's view of God and history did not satisfy me. It seemed to me that he did not make sufficient allowance for the meaningfulness of the people of God and for the complex interaction of the members of the body of Christ. Furthermore I began to see that the church was not only corporate but corporeal and that meaning was to be found not only in the Spirit of God but in the Body. Within the pages of the New Testament I found meaning given to the totality of creation not only to the imperishable essences. That was why the church baptized in water, ate and drank bread and wine, and held stubbornly to the doctrine of the resurrection of the body.

Step by step I was led to an interest in the doctrine of church (ecclesiology). I tried to understand the biblical and patristic views of the church. This led me into reviewing the meaning of the sacraments and into taking a second and more serious look at the history of the church. I even got drawn into liturgics and architecture.

My consideration of church history caused me to raise

questions about the periodic rebirth of the church—the meaning of awakening, rebirth, and conversion. What made the church alive? For several years I diligently gave myself to the topic of "convertive piety"—those individuals and movements who saw the renascence of the church as related to personal regeneration and commitment. I looked at the Anabaptists, the English Puritans, the German Pietists, the Moravians, and the followers of Wesley and Whitefield; I viewed the process of awakening in the American colonies, reading the sermons and treatises of American revivalists like Thomas Shepard, Jonathan Edwards, and Charles Finney. I saw the development of an Anglo-American evangelicalism in the nineteenth century with the major denominations, including such liturgical bodies as Lutherans and Episcopalians, at least informally stressing personal salvation, "the one thing needful." I devoted myself to the implications of the evangelism of Dwight L. Moody, Billy Sunday, Billy Graham, and a host of minor luminaries. I looked at the connections between evangelism and world missions. Finally I saw the development of the charismatic thrust in the present century and the parallel growth of Pentecostalism and Fundamentalism.

But I must confess to a disappointment. My professional studies of the Word of God, the People of God, and the Acts of God, and my efforts to communicate these truths resulted in the awakening of some intellectual interest and perhaps some modest inspiration. But I discovered that talking about the Bible and even trying seriously to teach it did not have the results I had hoped for. The same may be said for my efforts to present the new birth and the new life in Christ. No matter how in-

23

tense, rhetorical, and even polemical I became in the interest of "selling" the Bible and life in the Spirit, my hearers were largely unaffected. Some of the more honest ones accused me of special pleading, of defending the conservative establishment, and even of selling out to Fundamentalists. I can recall row upon row of chairs in the lecture hall occupied by both intellectually interested and bored and hostile beings.

What I did not see then but which has become more and more apparent to me is that faith may seek understanding, but understanding does not usually generate faith. A seminary may be a "seedbed" for ministerial apprentices or theological ideas; it is not generally a seedbed for life in the Spirit. This is not to reflect on intellectual disciplines. Thinking has a kind of inevitability. Faith will seek understanding. Logic can help to store the harvest when the seminal fury of spring and summer are past. But the more rational and orderly and logically systematic the church becomes, the smaller is its opportunity to bring faith to life. Reason and system can, of course, do many things. They can conquer the earth for the institution and, when coupled with wealth and political power, occupy the position of Dostoevsky's Grand Inquisitor. But they cannot often bring a soul to faith.

The church knows this. She has always known it. But she continues to translate faith or unfaith into objects which can be discussed and argued interminably. She presents the Bible—either intact as in evangelical circles or truncated as in liberal—as if it were facts or principles which a little more cleverness or a few more gimmicks could make palatable. A few months ago I saw a Bible study program for junior high school which presented

24

twelve and thirteen year olds with the textual theories of the Old Testament: J, P, E etc. I could not believe it. Textual criticism of this kind may help us to understand better the texture of Scriptural truth. But it is not, I should think, the way you initially interest adolescents in the Bible. I grope for a comparison. It is like beginning an art appreciation course by discussing what of Rubens was painted by his disciples or introducing Shakespeare by talking about pirated editions.

I am not trying to give professional study of the Bible a death blow or to depopulate the seminaries. I believe the seminaries have an indispensable function, if nothing other than to show the limits of human wisdom. My interest is rather to rescue the Bible for us or us for the Bible—to make the Scriptures once more the doorway to life.

But I am getting ahead of my story. In the middle 1960s when the theologians were meeting the need for freshness with the doctrine of the death of God, I was encountering a private despair. Intellectually I was re-examining the experiential base of Pietism. What I had formerly rejected as the error of a subjective theology, I now began to see as valid by its emphasis on the life in God.

In 1965 and 1966 I developed some lectures on Pietism in which I defended the much maligned doctrines of personal conversion, experiential faith, and an ordered lifestyle. I wanted to see life reborn—the sort of life in the spirit which I saw coursing through the church in the 18th and 19th centuries. Some years earlier I had written a brief peroration to a book on denominational history in which I had given voice to the same desire:

"Not only in the light of the past's triumphs, but in the face of today's struggles, the church was developing the will to have almost anything happen in order that life might come. It was willing to look at itself with cold clarity, to confess its humanity and sin: hardness of heart, presumption, vanity, lust, worldliness and greed, the filming over of intelligence, the thinning of emotion (no one weeps any more), the curious softening of the will. It was willing to pray once more with painful directness and without cant, 'Lord, be merciful!' It was willing to pray out of its ignorance the earth-shaking prayer of beginnings, 'Come, Holy Spirit!' in order that the prayer of consummation might once more have reality. 'Amen, come, Lord Jesus.' "

I wanted something to happen, and I talked about what I wanted and what I thought the church wanted. But inside I felt like Sisyphus pushing the interminable stone up the hill.

The Bible as Miracle

I guess that what I was waiting for was a miracle— God's pure act in time. I had believed through my youth and well into middle age that people could be persuaded to believe, and that I could persuade them. It was a deeply rooted conviction of mine that Christian rhetoric speaking to both intellect and will or feeling could bring people to faith. And I had devoted thirty or more years of my life to this kind of rhetoric. In speeches, sermons, lectures, articles, books, I had used every art of persuasion available to me to make the Christian gospel intellectually and aesthetically convincing and thus effective in bringing people to faith. I saw my audience as chiefly young intellectuals, turned off by the artistically clumsy and intellectually unconvincing message of the church. I wanted to do for them in a modest way what some great Christian intellectuals had done for me.

From 1959 to 1970 I was given the presidency of a fine liberal arts college and theological seminary, and I saw this as a laboratory where my ideas on Christian education could be worked out. I felt mandated by my gifted and devoted colleagues at the school as well as by the sponsoring denomination and its leadership. Perhaps my finest hour was the inaugural ceremony in which I stated as eloquently as I could the passion as well as the burden of my heart for the school. I said:

> How is it possible to attain the frosty excellence of a great educational institution and retain the holy idiocy of faith?
>
> We have the ambition to become a truly great school. Not a large school but a great one. Into this task we want to pour all that we have of imaginative vigor, intellectual acumen, and moral force. But we want also to embrace the freedom, the meekness, and the joyousness of faith.
>
> Who is equal to these things?

These are noble sentiments, and if sincere intentions would have been enough, the school, during the eleven years of my leadership, might have become a model Christian community. But I failed. I did not fail as the president of an educational institution, for I believe I did a tolerable job as an educator. But I failed as a Christian rhetorician. I ended my tenure as president without having won very many people to Christian discipleship.

Rebirth is God's miraculous act, and during my presidency and through my influence not many such miracles took place.

It was during this time that an executive of a nationally known publishing firm invited a handful of theologians and writers to a weekend of conversation about a theology for the laity. In the company of eagles I felt like a duck—web-footed and waddly. But I felt something more than awkwardness. I felt despair. Dialectical theology in the grand manner of Barth and Tillich had played out its option. In a curious way it was no longer interesting and exciting to these gifted men.

I remember saying very little, but on Sunday morning after some endless talk about the capacity or incapacity of the laity to grasp theological insights (I recall someone's dismissal of Robinson's *Honest to God* as a popular re-statement of what theologians had concluded decades earlier), my despair spoke for me. I said that I saw no renewal of the church in the laicizing of theology because it seemed to me that the theology of the theologians didn't have much faith or life to communicate. Perhaps, I concluded, the renewal of the church would have to emerge from the amniotic waters of store-front Pentecostals.

Just the other day I had a letter from a resident in psychiatry whose life and experience of grace fulfills the prophecy I uttered that dismal Sunday a decade ago, without really knowing what I was saying. He writes:

"I'm Jewish by birth, quite left-wing politically, very much involved in 'counter-culture' activities at the time Jesus barged into my life. I was at that time a senior in medical school about to begin a residency in psychiatry. (I'm now half-way through my second year of training.)

28

My exposure to drugs, sensitivity groups (from a distance), and much reading had led me far into the Eastern paths. I had dabbled in many areas, the I Ching, Zen, astrology (quite a bit), and finally Raja Yoga and the 'Self-Realization Fellowship' which was where I settled in.

"It just so happened Paramabansa Yogananda, the guru who started this organization, really grooved on Jesus—he thought Jesus was the greatest of gurus, and felt that the Bible was very similar to the Bhagavad-Gita—he was sort of into a universal life thing and tried to show how all religions were the same. Being a Jew I tripped over Jesus and fell flat on my face for quite a while—but one day as I was meditating I had a vision of a cross, and a few weeks later I had a reunion with a Jewish girl I had dated once. She had introduced me to Tarot cards, I Ching, acid, astrology, etc., and now she was telling me how she had 'met Jesus', and had recently been 'baptized in the Spirit' and spoken in tongues.

"A few weeks later I found my hippy-self in a tiny little Pentecostal church going forward. 'Jesus, if you really are who you say you are, and you can really show me God, I want you. Prove it to me.'

"Well, here I am, in the Lord for about twenty months and now that I've met Jesus, he is busily trying to help me to know me."

I did not then know that the renewal of my own faith lay around the corner and that its instrument would be not some definitive volume on the demise of God (although I must confess that this negative theology may have been God's way of thrusting me into a needful creative despair), but some ordinary people who brought me into a new relationship to God and myself and others.

It happened in 1967 at Laity Lodge in Texas, a place known to thousands through the ministries of Howard Butt, Keith Miller, Bill Cody, and scores of other Christian leaders.

I had been invited to give some talks on interpersonal relationships and in that capacity was also asked to lead a small group. I came into the group in the role of an expert—the person with the answers. But at some point during that week the members of my group, in a gentle but unmistakable way, brought me out of my role-playing into the novel reality of my own personhood. They told me what no one had ever said before in a way I could believe that it was OK to be me, that they loved Karl Olsson and not all that clanking armor of expertise I clomped around in.

The result was that I began, for the first time since childhood, to see people and to love them as people, and this vision pushed me back into the Bible.

There I discovered what I had never known in my guts —that the Bible is about relationships. In my Lutheran-Pietistic beginnings the relational had been largely limited to God's relationship to me. I was, of course, enjoined to love my neighbor, but that love was seen as a "secondary ethic," to use Barth's phrase. Now I began to perceive that relationships—in love—that is the relationship between people in God, was one thing, one ball of fragrant wax, promising both sweetness and light.

When accepted personally and relationally, the Bible, through the work of the Spirit, continually creates new relationships. It does not, like a listless phonograph needle, merely trace old grooves; it cuts fresh ones. It pushes me into an unending reassessment of my existence.

30

This is an exciting but terrifying experience, and I am sure that many will opt for something else. There are safer things than giving the Bible a personal, relational focus. Kierkegaard's story is not outdated. There is a room with two doors. Over one there is a sign, "Heaven"; on the other a sign "Lecture on Heaven." And people flock through the door to the lecture. It is safer to keep the Bible an object. If I do, I can worship it, attack it, or ignore it. But if I let the Bible become God's voice speaking to me and working in me, there is no escape, not even if I stick my fingers in my ears. I am on my way into the risk and beauty of salvation.

GROUP DESIGN 1

In groups of four, formed at random, have each participant divide a blank piece of paper into four squares. Label the first square ages 2-12; the second, 13-18; the third, 19-25; and the fourth, the present.

Have each person in the group draw a symbol in each square which expresses his or her religious feeling at that particular age level.

In the first square the participant may draw a symbol suggesting God as the starter of things, for example an old man with a beard. I would probably draw some trees because the Garden of Eden used to fascinate me. A friend of mine found himself drawing a flannelgraph as a religious symbol from ages 2-12. (By the way, it's OK to leave the square blank.)

In the second square the symbol may deal with the struggle with values, ideals, or rules, or with the search for security. The Bible may be felt as the Great Forbidder, a book of no-no's, or as a source of great strength or as a book which bores me or makes me important, or challenges me to be better or do better. The symbol might be the tables of the law or a police car or a great tree or rock, or as a remembrance from church, a picky suit or a choking necktie.

In the third square the symbol may suggest more specific intellectual and moral struggles: the need for or experience of guilt, forgiveness, and acceptance or the problem of faith and doubt. Some may want to draw a cross or a chapel or a lighted window or a dark cloud or some other object.

The symbol in the fourth square may deal with the unresolved tension or conflict of the present. Perhaps we struggle with a relationship with God, ourselves, significant others, or the world.

The focus of this design is to get at our feelings about the Bible, the church, and religious experience, both negative and positive.

When the symbols have been drawn, go around the circle and share the drawings and particularly what they mean in terms of feelings. We stress again that the purpose of the design is not to "sell" the Bible or the faith, but to share feelings about it—genuine, deep-down feelings.

2

THE KINGDOM
OF RIGHT
RELATIONSHIPS

Someone has called the kingdom of God the kingdom of right relationships, and it is here we begin our exploration of relational Bible study. I am indebted to my colleagues at Faith at Work for the sketch of the four relationships: God, self, significant others, and the world. To live relationally is to risk meaningful interaction with all four.

Four Relationships

What do I mean by meaningful interaction? Well, it is clear that in our ordinary contacts with God, ourselves, significant others, and the world, we often do what I have said we do with the Bible—we make everyone into an object, a thing. We approach God as if he were a target at whom we direct the arrows of our worship, petition, or intercession. Or we make him a character in a drama. Much has been made lately of the "mighty acts of God" as revealed in the Bible, and I want to honor that creative insight into the biblical vision of God. But the acting God can be as much of an object as the being God. I sit, like a spectator at a film, and see the God-events unroll.

I can also make myself into an object. I become a piece of external biography. Not long ago I asked an acquaintance to tell me about himself, by which I meant not how he saw himself in that item-by-item *Who's Who* we all carry around, but how he experienced himself at that moment. He proceeded to give me his biography. It was an extremely interesting piece of life, but hearing it narrated was like sitting at a movie. When it was over, the man was still opaque, like a monument on which important external things are inscribed but which finally tells you nothing about the inner man.

The "other" also easily becomes a thing, a wind-up doll whose every motion we can anticipate. It is the exceptional person who can tolerate an unpredictable friend. We like to surround ourselves with people who act predictably. Thus in every circle of friends there is a listing of the *dramatis personae:* Bill—Clown, Mary—Flirt, John—Chef, Dottie—Brain.

We act the parts of an old play, or we are in the seats watching. That is why the conversation so often has to do with other people, people who are out there. We feel safe when we can put down or ridicule someone outside the circle.

But in that kind of setting we cannot reveal who we are or pillory ourselves. It is not good form to bleed in public. The minute we expose our wound, our friends rush in with the band aids and the iodine. They are in a frenzy to put us back together. The clown must replace his mask, the flirt get back to work, the brain sizzle with insights and *bon mots.*

In relation to the world I play a similar game. Instead of relating to the world by getting a bite-size piece of the action, I think cosmically. The world's problems are magnified as on a universal screen, and I sit back and rail at people (including myself) for letting these things happen. I make the problems political rather than personal and believe that the solutions too are entirely political. If we can only get that candidate or that party elected into office, the problem will be solved and I need no longer feel accountable.

In discussing the relationships, I have deliberately availed myself of the language of the theater and the film. I have spoken of our roles as those of actors or spectators. I have done this because I believe that this is the way most of us handle our relationships. We objectify and depersonalize ourselves and others.

By doing this we manage to avoid relationships. For these are possible only between persons. Lloyd Ogilvie has called our attention to the way in which we "thing" people. That is, we change them from self-initiating persons into objects we can control and manipulate. "Thinging it" with God and people keeps us from dealing with our own feelings and the feelings of others and thus insulates us from the pain of relationships.

But when we interact personally, everything undergoes a "sea change into something rich and strange." Nothing stays in the places we have assigned. God comes alive and presses in upon us in a chain of creative charities; we in turn become alive and interact in terms of feeling and will. Like Job and Moses and the psalmists and Jesus and Paul we carry on a hot conversation with the Most High. We thank him, but we also question him, plead with him, get angry with him, turn our backs on him, dare to stay unreconciled with him, even doubt his existence in a fury of bafflement—and also in trust commend ourselves to him.

And my self is no longer a finished and packaged thing. I am every stage of being, telescoped but active: the infant, the child, the adolescent, the adult. I can taste my tears and feel the fires of my lust; I can rejoice in my integrity, my human "me-ness" and at the same time deplore the grubby, scratching, smelly creature I am. Carl Sandburg talks of the wolf and the fox in him. It's easier for me to see myself as a melancholy ape swinging from leafless branches above the mire and the peanut shells—a crotchety baboon, but a baboon dreaming of being an angel, and looking out wistfully through simian eyes on the balloons and the summer faces.

But because I am like that and can see myself like that, I can commune with the other. The other is no longer a formidable being, playing big daddy and trying to terrify me into obedient servitude or a docile child letting me big-daddy him; the other is a person of "like nature with me" as Paul and Barnabas once told the Lystrans. Which means that we can confess to one another, listen to one another, absolve one another, and pray for one another.

When viewed relationally, the world ceases to be so big that I have no responsibility for it. The world is my doorstep. The world is the person unknown to me whom I allow to minister to me. It is the cup of cold water not only given but received in Jesus' name. The big revolution in that relationship will come when we fat, fair western Christian superstars let the world relate to us by helping us, not in colonial submission, but in the dignity and freedom of their personhood.

Four Principles

Coming to the Bible personally and relationally means that suddenly the operatic stage with all its trappings of camels and asses, horses and warriors, tents and caravans, priests in absurd headgear and prophets in breechclouts— suddenly all this antique claptrap is transformed into a mirror. I am the man. It's my book. It's God's word to me—to us. Wow!

To make this a little clearer I suggest four principles of relational Bible study that have proved helpful to me. In offering these I have no illusions about saying anything novel or startling, for these principles have informed homiletics for a long time. Puritan homileticians three centuries ago used to talk about the "application" of the sermon, the part that was to hit home, and this is more or less what we are dealing with.

If there is any difference between conventional Bible study and what we are talking about, it lies in the manner of presentation. Relational Bible study is not something to be taught and studied. It is not a preacher or teacher giving content to students, pouring a full notebook into an empty one. It is people looking together into a mirror and finding their lives reflected. Relational Bible study is a vision of myself in relationship. Hence it leads to no programmed result. It may bring me to conversion, but it may not. It is distressingly open-ended. Unlike the well-prepared sermon or Bible study which never fails because failure is programmed out, the relational Bible study may fall flat on its face and speak to no one. And that has to be OK too.

The first principle of relational Bible study is to make

37

the story my story. This means being willing to enter into the magnetic field of the character and incidents as if they concerned me. In a great deal of evangelical preaching the sermon is directed to the goodies or the baddies, the converted or unconverted. Once I am in the converted category, I need no longer take evangelistic preaching with the same seriousness. It is really not my story. Of course, this is an oversimplification, for I know few converted people who really feel thoroughly converted. Hence a stout evangelistic sermon is sure to hit a lot of people in both camps. But a relational Bible study doesn't offer me the same option. To give myself to it, to make it my story, means that I do not have any neat little immunities. I cannot, like Dante in the Inferno, be unsinged by the fires, or like an astronaut, walk around in a safe space suit. The Bible becomes me.

Let us take, as an example, a familiar story from Luke's Gospel: the visit of Jesus to Jericho and his encounter with Zacchaeus. The story unfolds like the scenes of a movie. I see the dusty road along which Jesus comes walking, surrounded by his intimates and the crowd of stray followers. And I see the main tree-lined street of Jericho beginning to fill up with people who are anxious to see the wonder-working street preacher from Galilee. And I see Zacchaeus looking around for a place where he can see what is about to happen and finally climbing up into the sycamore tree.

But where am I in the story? As I personally think about it, I am not in the story at all. The events are taking place on a picture-frame stage or on a movie screen, and I am about to dip my hand in the box for another mouthful of popcorn.

But to make the passage my story means that I feel not only the excitement of that long vanished scene but the deep need for Jesus and his ministry that must have surfaced among the people as our Lord approached the city. More than that I feel my own need of him.

The second principle I would suggest is that we identify with a character in the story. This will be the person we feel closest to at the moment. It may be the Prodigal or the Elder Brother in the parable, Peter or Thomas among the disciples, Zacchaeus, Jairus, Mary, Martha, Cornelius, Saul, Ananias of Damascus, Barnabas. It may be a person without a name. The important thing is not to dress up in first century Palestinian clothes but to feel what the biblical person feels.

This immediately involves relationships. The Bible is a book about them. The very first story in the Old Testament has to do with Adam's relationship to Eve and their relationship to God; the same pattern holds true throughout. Let us continue with the story of Zacchaeus as an example. This seems to concern only the relationship between Jesus and Zacchaeus but more is involved. For Zacchaeus is what he is because of his relationship to the world around him. He is the chief tax collector in that area. In first century Palestine this meant something much worse than, let us say, an employee of the Internal Revenue Service. In Jesus' day and under Roman occupation the chief tax job was sold to the highest bidder. He was responsible for returning a portion of what he collected to the government; the rest was his to keep. Thus the job provided an opportunity for all sorts of unethical deals. Extortion, fraud, and questionable accounting were not unusual. Zacchaeus was known by his fellow townsmen in Jericho as a "sinner."

He seems not to have been honest, but even if he had been scrupulously so, he might still have drawn down on himself the ill will of the community. It is not easy to be a public servant, and Zacchaeus could not have found it so. All those who assume responsibility for leadership —politicians, parents, employers, supervisors, clergymen, union agents, athletic managers, artists and performers of various kinds—are by virtue of their roles open to hostility and criticism. Anyone who lives in the relationships involved in leadership can thus identify with Zacchaeus.

But more is involved. For leadership, even though superficially honest, carries with it a burden of miscellaneous guilt. No leader escapes the uneasy feeling that he has used and manipulated those he is called to serve. Even though he may have the best intentions, the people with whom he lives and works easily become objects and roles rather than persons. Here too it is possible to identify with the Jericho tax collector.

Finally we see in Zacchaeus' story a most important detail. It highlights the man's relationship to himself. Zacchaeus was a little man. And little men must try very hard to add a cubit to their stature. But very quickly we move beyond physical dimensions. For who is not a little man? Inside we are all small of stature. Hence all of us look for a sycamore tree to give us elevation, to lift us above the crowd. In our insecurity we may want to feel like Friedrich Nietzsche's Superman, or like the poet, Elinor Wylie, who writes:

Avoid the reeking herd,
Shun the polluted flock,
Live like that stoic bird,
The eagle of the rock.

But we are still little people to ourselves.

As I write this, I blush to remember the many ways in which I have personally climbed into sycamore trees to get above the crowd: name-dropping, a touch of expertise, an allusion to a book or journal or newspaper with relevance and style, a pushing forward of a relative or family member who is "making it," proving someone wrong about a fact or principle, parlaying one's money—however limited—into some kind of privilege.

John Updike has a poem about an intellectual who goes to a party with some fellow intellectuals. On the way home he reviews his performance:

Was I clever enough? Was I charming?
Did I make at least one good pun?
Was I disconcerting? Disarming?
Was I wise? Was I wan? Was I fun?

Did I answer that girl with white shoulders
Correctly, or should I have said
(Engagingly), "Kierkegaard smolders,
But Eliot's ashes are dead"?

And did I, while being a smarty,
Yet some wry reserve slyly keep,
So they murmured, when I'd left the party,
"He's deep. He's deep. He's deep"?

It is all so familiar, so human, and so sad.

The third principle of relational Bible study is to find the gospel. A great deal of preaching is adept at finding the message or the moral of a text. We are such excellent teachers. Like John the Baptist we tell people what to do. "Now, if I were you, I would. . . ." When tax collectors came to John the Baptist to be baptized and asked him, "Teacher, what shall we do?" John said, "Collect no more than is appointed you." In other words, "Repent." This is a good word. The world needs its prophets and advisers, its Ann Landers and its Abby Van Buren. But John's word is not gospel.

When Jesus meets Zacchaeus, he does not lay a new moral burden on him. I am sure that Zacchaeus already was weighed down by all the spiritual and ethical demands the righteous community had laid on his back. Hence Jesus does not teach Zacchaeus. He does not offer to convert him or change him or challenge him. He simply affirms him. And he does this by asking something quite ordinary of him.

Our temptation, when we want to be helpful to people, is to offer them something we have. We might assume, since Jesus is the Savior, that on this occasion he will offer Zacchaeus forgiveness. Forgiveness is Jesus' business, said Heinrich Heine, and the tax collector certainly needed it. But Jesus does not offer anything. He asks for something. In effect, he asks for an invitation to dinner. And he does not do this in a patronizing way, as when we sometimes ask a moppet for a piece of his sticky candy. He asks out of need, as when he turned to the little boy for his lunch of bread and fish.

And this is the gospel. The gospel is the unbelievable truth that God thinks each one of us important enough to come to us. The gospel is not only that we need God but that God needs us and is willing to trust us even though we fail him again and again.

The fourth principle is to give the story a name. By this I mean summing up the passage in a telling picture or metaphor. My friend and colleague, Heidi Frost of Faith at Work, calls the Zacchaeus story "How to Kiss a Frog."

Summing up the passage in this way gives each hearer an open-ended script for which he can fill in the blanks. It provides a handle. Bruce Larson's Bible study on Jesus' raising Lazarus has the title, "Unwrapping Lazarus." I have called the parable of the Prodigal Son, "Come to the Party."

Giving the story a name thus does more than dress up such abstract terms as *conversion* and *regeneration* in figurative language. The name or metaphor makes the generalization particular and thrusts it down to a level of consciousness where flow the springs of feeling and will. When presented as a witness to my particular experience, that is by modeling, it may make the hearer *want* to have his froginess kissed, or to be unwrapped from all the hangups that wrap him, or to go the party forever. It may make him want to be a new person and live in a new world.

I think it can thus be argued that "giving the story a name" is, under the guidance and in the power of the Holy Spirit, a truly creative or recreative act. It may make people over, transforming them into new creatures in Christ Jesus.

I have just been reading Owen Barfield's little book, *Poetic Diction: A Study in Meaning.* Barfield claims that the poet has not merely the function of holding the mirror up to nature, that is, passively reflecting the brokenness and waste of the time; he has also the function of "making

43

meaning," of turning existence around and endowing it with fresh significance. In writing about the reflective, passive tendency in Hardy and Eliot, Barfield writes:

> Accordingly they [the modern poets] have presented us with the human spirit as bewildered observer, or as agonized patient, compassionate in Hardy, humbled or repentant in Eliot, but always the observer, always the patient, helpless to alter anything but his own pin-pointed subjective emotion.

I think God intends more than that and has through his Word and Spirit given us power to achieve more than that. Witness, for example, the new world created in the midst of the brokenness and waste of despairing young people by the Jesus movement or the new spirit of expectancy which breathes in the lyrics and music of Black America.

Without in any way ignoring the complexity and evil of the human situation, I believe that the Word and the Spirit can and do create a new world inside and outside ourselves. It is to this miracle we are invited by the biblical word.

GROUP DESIGN 2

In groups of four read *one* of the following stories:

> The Paralyzed Man: Mark 2:1-12
> The Good Samaritan: Luke 10:25-37
> Mary and Martha: Luke 10:38-42

1. Have each member of the group try to identify with a character in the story.
2. When everyone in the group has done this, ask each one to state the good news for him in the passage.

3

THE RISK
OF
RELATIONSHIPS

Our time is caught between the upper and nether mill-
stones of security and risk. We have a growing chorus
of prophets urging us to be more cautious. Ralph Nader
and his disciples point out the hazards in cyclamates, automobiles, fried chicken, drinking water, and smog. The
Surgeon General tells us about the perils of cigarette
smoking. Colored TV tubes are supposed to give us can-
cer; so are licorice, cranberries, barbecued meat, hair spray,
deodorants, sun tan oils, pipe stems, and birth control
pills.

On the other hand we are being urged to live a riskier
life. We invent and produce more and more engines of
potential destruction: water skis, snowmobiles, gliders,
diving gear, dune buggies, motorcycles, indecently powerful automobiles, private planes. We discover, manufacture,
and market a host of drugs to produce the precise mood
and temper we want and risk our life and sanity in con-
suming them. It is not only the young who are hooked
on dope and booze. Despite the risks, America as a whole
is a nation of pill-eaters, alcohol guzzlers, and voracious
consumers of tobacco.

Creative Risk

It's hard to know who will win out, the Naders or the riskers. But whatever the outcome, most people, whether timid or rash, will probably avoid the most creative risk of all—that of relationships. In some ways it is easier to join a mountain-climbing expedition than to work out my relationships with my family or colleagues. In fact, as was evident recently when an international mountain climbing team attempted Everest, the physical and technical problems proved insignificant in contrast to the relational difficulties within the team.

The struggle to establish relationships begins early, and it doesn't take much to tip the scales. A few experiences of rejection or ridicule (which is a kind of rejection) and the child begins to develop a tough protective covering.

I could not have been more than three when I went with my mother to her home community in south-central Sweden. One morning we went to visit some neighbors. The men were at work, and the room was filled with only women. I recall seeing myself surrounded by knees. One of the women in the room was nursing a child, and the sight of the bared breast embarrassed me furiously. My face became flaming red and I hid myself in my mother's skirt. The sturdy peasant women noticed my discomfiture and found it hilarious. They hooted with laughter. They asked if I was jealous and wanted a taste. I found the teasing and the ridicule impossible to handle. I began to scream and kick, and my mother had to carry me from the room. I remember the incident because it made me develop scar tissue. With those women at least I would never again allow my feelings to show. My sophistication had begun.

Thus very early in life and regardless of our station in society we crawl into a diversity of roles which, like turtle shells, protect our vulnerable humanity. We fear to be seen as we are and to be known as we are. Like medieval castellans we pull up the drawbridge to keep ourselves away from people and to keep people away from us. And because we are so afraid of relationships we let all sorts of gifts "fust in us unused."

Risk in the Gospel

It was characteristic of Jesus to run the risks of relationship. He selected his disciples without any careful screening of their powers or hang-ups. And he dealt with other people in the same direct, incautious way. Let us look at one of these risky encounters recorded for us in Luke's Gospel (7:36ff TEV):

A Pharisee invited Jesus to have dinner with him. Jesus went to his house and sat down to eat. There was a woman in that house who lived a sinful life. She heard that Jesus was eating in the Pharisee's house, so she brought an alabaster jar full of perfume and stood behind Jesus by his feet, crying and wetting his feet with her tears. Then she dried his feet with her hair, kissed them, and poured the perfume on them. When the Pharisee who had invited Jesus saw this, he said to himself, "If this man really were a prophet, he would know who this woman is who is touching him; he would know what kind of sinful life she leads!" Jesus spoke up and said to him, "Simon, I have something to tell you." "Yes, Teacher," he said, "tell me." "There were two men who owed money to a moneylender," Jesus began; "one owed him five hundred dollars and the other one fifty dollars. Neither one could pay him back, so he cancelled the debts of both. Which one, then, will love him more?" "I suppose," answered Simon, "that it was the one who was forgiven more." "Your answer is correct," said Jesus. Then he turned to the woman and said to Simon: "Do you see this woman? I came into your home, and you gave me no water for my feet, but she has washed my feet with her tears and dried them with her hair. You did not welcome me with a kiss, but she has not stopped kissing my feet since I came. You provided no oil for my head, but she has covered my feet with perfume. I tell you, then, the great love she has shown proves that her many sins have been forgiven. Whoever has been forgiven little, however, shows only a little love." Then Jesus said to the woman, "Your sins are forgiven." The others sitting at the table began to say to themselves, "Who is this, who even forgives sins?" But Jesus said to the woman, "Your faith has saved you; go in peace."

The story of this interesting triangle—Simon, Jesus, and the prostitute—gives us examples of risk-taking. Let us review the situation. Simon, a Pharisee and respected member of the community, has invited a young street preacher named Jesus to his house for lunch. Simon has a flair for inviting newsworthy people, and this particular week Jesus is certainly the celebrity. Jesus has accepted the invitation and is reclining at the luncheon table when a prostitute enters and makes her way to his side.

Medium Risk

Let's look at the intruder. She is a prostitute, apparently successful in her trade, for she has bought a flask of some expensive perfume for the occasion. Her actions show remarkable courage. For although her clientele is men, this situation is novel for her. In bringing her gift to Jesus she risks not only the scorn of the community and the rejection of Simon; she must also penetrate the security guard assembled around Jesus.

We know from other stories that many people who tried to get to see Jesus were stopped by his friends. Their motives were probably mixed. On the one hand they wanted to save Jesus from wearying interruptions. They particularly wanted to relieve him of the harassment of the little people who crossed his path: lunatics, beggars, the insistent sick, troublesome children. But on the other hand, they wanted to be sure that they had a large slice of Jesus for themselves.

But the woman braves more than outward circumstances. She has her own insecurity to deal with as well as her fear that Jesus may misunderstand. The song of Mary Magdalene in *Jesus Christ Superstar* "I Don't Know How to Love Him," tells the story. When we don't know how to love people or what to do for them, the easiest tactic is to withdraw. But the woman's need—and certainly her love—was greater than her fear. And so she risked rejection, misunderstanding, scorn—in short, a fiasco—to push her way to the side of Jesus.

Low Risk

The second member of the triangle is Simon, the Pharisee. We know almost nothing about him. The Gospels give us rather one-sided pictures of the adversaries of Jesus, and we don't normally have kindly feelings toward either Sadducees or Pharisees. But Simon was not a bad man or even a cowardly one. He seems to have had enough courage to give lunches for celebrities who passed through the city, even officially suspected or at least unpopular ones like Jesus. We honor him for that.

But he didn't want to overdo the risking. For example, he did not want to be thought an intimate of Jesus. Hence he omitted the tokens of hospitality: water for his feet, oil for his hair and beard, the kiss of greeting. He is also aware of how the intrusion of the unholy woman may affect his image in the town. He doesn't throw her out (perhaps because he doesn't want to touch her), but he dissociates himself from her.

High Risk

The third character in the drama is Jesus himself. The figure of our Lord has been so overlaid with bad, if pious, art; with moral cliches of superhuman goodness, serenity, and sweetness; or with theological *a priori* throughout the centuries that we read even the Gospels through the eyes of Hoffman and Plockhorst. It is almost impossible to strip him down to the essential humanity he must have presented to his followers. A work like *Jesus Christ Superstar,* though it leaves a lot out, has the advantage of being written by people who came to their work fresh. Hence their Jesus, though he may be inaccurate, has the virtue of being human.

If Jesus was human, there must have been a sense in which he wanted to make it, not only with Simon, but with the other people in the town. He was not a masochist who had a sick need to suffer. He was not antisocial, indifferent to the abuse and rejection of people. He was human in a beautiful, healthy way, and every critical encounter must have brought him pain.

Is it irreverent to think of Jesus as being initially embarrassed by the presence of this woman? This is certainly a men's party, and when the woman enters, Jesus is reclining with Simon at the head table. We must not think of her as a magnificent, well-groomed redhead, the favorite of a Roman master sergeant in the tradition of Cecil B. DeMille, but as an anonymous and perhaps undistinguished plier of her trade.

But whatever her appearance, her profession was obvious, and in Jesus' place we may well have been both embarrassed and distressed by her presence.

Should he ignore her? Should he greet her politely and send her on her way? Should he accept her caresses but not their seductive intent? While these possibilities crowd the mind of Jesus, the woman comes to the couch where he is reclining. She weeps out of fear, out of guilt, out of love. The text does not explain. And as the tears fall from her eyes, they wet the feet of Jesus. In a gesture of loneliness and love, she takes her hair and wipes his feet. Then she kisses them and pours perfume on them. All of these acts are ambivalent. They are acts of hospitality unperformed by Simon. But they are also signals to the senses. Performed by a prostitute, they have an unmistakably erotic character. They are tricks of the woman's profession. This is a trade language known around the world and the only dialect in which she can communicate with men. But this is all she has, and in an act of impulsive generosity she risks it for Jesus.

The beautiful thing is that Jesus lets her be. He does not

back off or pull his feet up under his robe. He doesn't play coy or send her away. He doesn't look around nervously to see if anyone is watching. He doesn't ask for a Bible or suggest that they pray together. He doesn't teach or preach. He does not try to straighten her out. He lets her be.

The risk is obvious. To be associated with sinners is one thing; to be identified with them and seemingly conniving with them in their sin is something else. Some ministers have a ministerial way of dealing with risky people. It is self-conscious or priggish or collusive. But Jesus is himself. He thus runs the full risk. He lets her love him in her way, the only way she knows, and he accepts the consequences.

Consequences of Risking

Some of these suggest themselves to us. He may have been thought naive—a Brother Juniper or Alyosha whose innocence protected him. Simon apparently thought of Jesus in these terms. He said in effect, "What is this man thinking of? He's a prophet and should be able to see through her. But he doesn't." We can get out of some situations by playing dumb. But Jesus does not take that route.

Worse yet, he may have been thought sophisticated. Some may have suspected that he was using his religious role to turn people to his uses. The cynical mind is always ready to charge the loving person with questionable motives.

There must also have been people in that room who saw quite clearly that Jesus was neither naive nor cynical but open and loving. And that truth would have been devastating to them.

Despite these reactions, Jesus affirms the woman and gives public witness to his affirmation. He contrasts her love with that of Simon—a hazardous thing to do.

Textual critics have been troubled by the intrusion of the short parable into the text. It is the parable of the two debtors whose debts are of very different amounts but who are both released from their obligations. The question is asked, "Is Jesus saying that the forgiven know how to love, or that those who love are forgiven, or that the believing and risking attain forgiveness?" It seems to me that he is saying all three. The woman and Jesus have entered an arena where love insures forgiveness and forgiveness generates love. Both enter this experience by risking, that is by faith. Simon the Pharisee's problem is that he does not want to enter the experience in any significant way. Because of his fears he remains a spectator. He risks virtually nothing and thus does not have an authentic encounter with either Jesus or the woman.

Roles and Risking

Which brings us to where we are in the matter of risking something for a relationship. Many of us avoid the personal by staying shut up in a role. We justify our distance from people by claiming that this is what parents or doctors or lawyers or teachers or pastors must do. This is the only way we keep control. And, of course, this is true. If Jesus had been a rabbi to the unholy woman, he would have kept control and saved himself trouble.

I am a novice in the realm of right relationships. Sometimes I feel that I will never learn to be personal. I have spent a good part of my life playing one role or another. I have taken many professional risks, but it is just lately that I have wanted to take the risk of being personal and human.

Let me tell you about an experience. I was invited to a parish to help celebrate the hundredth anniversary of the founding of the church. It was a great occasion. I believe I was invited because in my professional capacity of a church historian I knew something about the place. My expertise would grace the occasion and add splendor to the whole. I was to be one of the wise old men of the tribe bringing his blessing to the party.

But I was lonely in my expertise. I wanted to enter the celebration as a guest among other guests and not as a pundit. On Saturday night there was a hundredth anniversary party, and I tried to make my way in. I walked from group to group, but I was special in some curious way, and people backed off.

The next morning it was my privilege to preach the anniversary sermon. I think I know what was expected— an immortal word to sum up the meaning of 100 years of toil and triumph. But instead of trying to preach that kind of sermon, I gave a personal witness on the meaning of grace. I talked about the fact that God became man in Jesus to be with people, and in spite of our many hang-ups most of us want to be people to people. I also referred to my experience of loneliness the night before. Then I did something very risky for me and for that setting. I asked the congregation to sing the hymn, "Amazing Grace." I suggested that during the singing of the hymn those who wanted to might turn to look at their neighbor in the pew. I was sure, I said, that some might rather look at their vest buttons or purse handles than at the person next to them and if they felt that way, it was OK.

While I was giving the instructions, I thought of how dumb a thing this was to do. And how it put me on the spot. Because now, obviously, I would have to walk down among the people and look at them while we sang.

I was terrified. I had memories from my childhood of evangelists who "pew fished" on Sunday nights in search of converts. I disliked this forced intimacy, the indelicate invasion of the privacy of people. And now, in a sense, I was doing the same thing.

I also had some very practical fears. I said to myself, "What if I look at people and they won't look at me? And what will they think of me? A former professor and seminary administrator making a fool of himself as if he had suffered softening of the brain or become a ham actor over night?"

I warred within myself. I hated to take the step. But in the last minute I took it. I walked down the aisle during the singing of the hymn, and with my heart racing I looked right and left into the faces of the people. I wanted to drop through the floor. But as I walked I was rewarded. People did not turn away. A few shy or angry ones looked at their vest buttons and purse handles, but many, yes most, turned toward their neighbors and toward me smiling warmly and even weeping.

At the end of the service a large man came up to me and said, "I am sure I am the man who backed away from you last night. I was afraid of you because you were supposed to be the guest speaker. But now it's OK and I just want to be your friend." And he gave me a bear hug.

The more I read about Jesus, the more I understand that the big risk is not the flight into space or the climbing of Everest, but looking into the eyes of another person and reaching out my hand to him and affirming our common humanity. In such risking there is healing and blessing.

But there is also embarrassment. As I write this, I think of that Sunday morning and ask myself if I wasn't a fool. I am sure many people who were there think I was. I tend to agree with them. But there is no way around the problem. To risk is to crank in the possibility of failure and embarrassment. To risk is to live with cold sweat and the blush of confusion and the pain of rejection. To risk is to war with your memories because everything does not turn out all right. To risk is to be a fool for Christ's sake. And I have to learn that this too is OK.

GROUP DESIGN 3

In groups of three or four, formed at random but perhaps not first-timers in small group sharing, have each person deal with the following questions:

1. With what one person am I able to risk sharing myself most freely and why? Even with that person what do I find myself withholding? Something that, if revealed, would hurt him or would lessen his estimate of me?

2. With what one person who is important to me do I

need to risk an encounter? What holds me back? Some frailty in him? Or some insecurity in me?

3. What specific steps can I take to make an encounter with this person effective?

4. On what resources can I draw in facing this risk-filled encounter? Prayer? Sharing with one other person or with my small group?

If the situation does not initially make this a promising group design, it may be helpful to have each participant answer the questions in a notebook or journal before sharing them with his group. This helps to clarify feelings and, when needed, provides practical limits for sharing.

4

HOW CAN
GOD USE
MY GAME PLAN?

My colleague Bruce Larson once asked me if I had thought about the fact that, like professional football teams readying for a game, most people operate by a "game plan." That is, most people have a persistent strategy with which they respond to situations of stress. Bruce's questions set some wheels spinning in me. I recalled a question Bill Pannell raises, "What is the point of your story?" And I remembered that Aristotle's definition of character is choice. The things a person in a drama presistently chooses to do constitute his character, according to the Greek philosopher.

Assuming for a moment that such a game plan exists in most of us, let us look together at a familiar text from Mark's Gospel: the story of Jesus and his three friends on the mount of transfiguration (9:2-8 TEV).

> Six days later Jesus took Peter, James, and John with him and led them up a high mountain by themselves. As they looked on, a change came over him, and his clothes became shining white, whiter than anyone in the world could wash them. Then the three disciples saw Elijah and Moses, who were talking with Jesus. Peter spoke up and said to Jesus, "Teacher, it is a good thing that we are here. We

will make three tents, one for you, one for Moses, and one for Elijah." He and the others were so frightened that he did not know what to say. A cloud appeared and covered them with its shadow, and a voice came from the cloud, "This is my own dear Son—listen to him!" They took a quick look around but did not see anyone else; only Jesus was with them.

The text we have read is familiar to most sermon hearers. The transfiguration experience is seen as a point of high inspiration which three of the disciples of Jesus were privileged to share, and the text is applied by contrasting the transfiguration mountain with the valley below. The argument runs something like this: there are moments of high inspiration in life, but once they are over we must learn to return to the valley with its burdens and responsibilities.

I would like to take a different view of the text. For me the heart of the story is not inspiration, but the transfiguration of Jesus. In the English language the word transfiguration suggests a *change in form or appearance*. Such a transformation did of course take place. The synoptic Gospels are agreed that the clothes of Jesus became very shining and white, and two of the Gospels speak also of the transformation of his face into a kind of radiance. But the deeper meaning of the word transfiguration is *clarification*. In some sense the life and ministry of Jesus and his impending death and resurrection are summed up in the mountain experience. In it we see for the first time what it is all about. One way of putting it is that here for the first time we see Jesus' game plan, his strategy, or his character fully revealed.

Jesus' Game Plan

This may be the meaning of his mysterious encounter on the mountain with the figures of Moses and Elijah, who for the Jewish people represented the most sacred parts of the Scriptures—the law and the prophets. Luke tells us that Moses and Elijah, who also appeared in their heavenly glory, talked with Jesus about "how he would soon fulfill God's purpose by dying in Jerusalem." The mount of transfiguration thus became the scene of Jesus' stepping into his historic role as the suffering servant and the Messiah, a role prophesied in the Old Testament. Put another way, here was revealed God's total game plan anticipated in the Old Testament figures and fulfilled in Jesus. Hence, the meaning of the voice from the cloud, "This is my own dear Son—listen to him!"

Far from "inspirational" in the ordinary sense—a word which makes us think of eloquent preaching or triumphant singing—this was a time of such overwhelming clarity and truth that its effect on the disciples was to terrify them, literally to scare them out of their wits. It is in this context that we must judge the response of Simon Peter. We have already said that it is in moments of stress or crisis that we reveal our basic game plan. And this is certainly true of Peter at this point. I have never been able to make much sense of Peter's impulsive suggestion that he together with the other disciples be allowed to build three tents or booths for the three very important persons. The usual reasoning is that Peter was so overwhelmed by the beauty of the occasion that he wanted to keep it forever. Only when we read the text more carefully do we discover that in at least two of the Gospel accounts Peter comes forward with this suggestion because he is frightened. Mark says he and the others were so frightened that he did not know what to say, and Luke reports almost the identical fact.

Peter's Game Plan

Thus Peter's strange suggestion of the booths must be seen as the revelation of his character under intense stress. He is very frightened, and he reveals his game plan. There are not many sustained narratives about Peter in the Gospels or in Acts, but there are significant glimpses. These tell us two things about Peter: he was easily frightened and he responded to moments of fright by trying to take charge. That was his game plan. From the very first moment we encounter him until the last glimpse of him in the Epistles of the New Testament, Peter remains a "take-charge" person. Let us look at a few episodes.

In Matthew 16 we are told that Jesus began to reveal his game plan to his disciples: "I must go to Jerusalem and suffer much from the elders and the chief priests, and the teachers of the Law. I will be put to death, and on the third day I will be raised to life." Peter's responses was to take the Lord aside and say to him, "God forbid it, Lord! This must never happen to you!"

On the night in which Jesus was betrayed Peter tells Jesus that although the rest of the disciples flee, he will remain steadfast. Later the same evening he reveals his take-charge character by striking off the ear of the servant of the High Priest, Malchus, with a sword. Even the disastrous following of Jesus into the court yard of the high priest may be seen as part of Peter's game plan. We may be sure that he followed the Lord because he truly loved him, but there is also something of the aggressive leadership role in Peter's act. Matthew says that Peter went into the court yard to see how it would all come out. We remember that it came out very badly and that Peter only succeeded in denying his Lord—a bitterly painful experience for the loyal, brash, and inevitably cowardly disciple.

We might assume that after the death and resurrection of Jesus and his encounter with the Lord on the shore of Lake Tiberius Peter would change his game plan and become a different person, but this is not the case. He remains until the end of his life a "take-charge" person. This is clear from the little vignette we get of Peter's visit to Antioch during Paul's ministry there. The story is told in Galatians 2:11-15. Paul tells us that while he behaved toward the Gentile Christians with true freedom, Peter vacillated and, under pressure from some Jewish Christians, refused to continue his association with Gentile believers. Paul writes that the other Jewish brothers started acting like cowards along with Peter and that even Barnabas was swept along by their cowardly actions. Paul writes, "When I saw that they were not walking a straight path in line with the truth of the gospel, I said to Peter in front of them all: 'You are a Jew, yet you have been living like a Gentile, not like a Jew. How then can you try to force Gentiles to live like Jews?' " (TEV).

In this attack on Peter and his cowardice Paul reveals his own game plan, a plan that becomes clear in one form or another throughout his Epistles as well as in the Book of Acts. Paul's game plan was "to straighten people out," and he uses this strategy frequently in dealing with the churches he has established.

Our Various Game Plans

Turning now from the game plan of Peter and Paul let us look for a moment at ourselves. Under conditions of stress how do we characteristically react? What is our strategy and game plan? I have listed a few possibilities, but I am sure there are many. In fact, every person may have one or more game plans. This is my partial list:

1. Panic and withdraw.
2. Take over and manage. Propose a plan of action. Do something. Appoint a committee.
3. Straighten people out. Criticize and blame others for the situation. Write a letter to the newspaper.
4. Try to make everybody happy.
5. Do nothing. Stand very still and hope that the problem will go away.
6. Creatively undergo. Get involved. Suffer.
7. Insist on belonging, on being part of the action. Play a supportive role. Ride in the ambulance if necessary to stay with the action.
8. Begin by refusing to participate and then reconsider and enter in.
9. Begin by overcommitting yourself to the situation and withdraw when you see that you lack resources.
10. Intellectualize. Find reasons for what has happened or project an outcome. Find comfort in how many people have had the same experience or how few.
11. Moralize: "This has happened because some moral principle was violated. This always happens when. . . ."
12. Blame yourself. Identify yourself as the cause of disaster or as its victim.
13. Talk. Verbalize. Keep repeating the story of what happened as if that would solve the problem.
14. Minimize: "It can't be this bad."

15. Exaggerate: "It's so bad, the world is coming to an end."
16. Nourish: Bring a casserole.

My Own Game Plan

I would like to tell you about one of my game plans because it is not unlike that of Simon Peter. When I feel insecure or frightened, my game plan is to take over. I don't normally run away. I just begin to plan and manage.

During World War II Myron Madden and I were both stationed in England waiting for our division to move across the channel. The invasion of Europe had already begun, and we received first-hand reports from the combat zone which filled us with horror. I remember saying to Myron, "If that is what combat is like, as soon as the going gets rough I can see myself running across the field like a scared rabbit." In the weeks prior to our embarkation for the continent I lived with deep anxiety and depression because I was sure I would respond to fear by flight. I did not understand myself very well, for when we did eventually get into combat, I responded to my fear by taking charge. When things got tough, in the midst of my panic, I managed. I helped set up medical aid stations. I coordinated the evacuation of the wounded. I even dispersed vehicles under artillery and air attack. And I did not do these things because I was a hero but because I was a manager. My game plan was to be in charge.

Twenty-five years later I was still using the same game plan. On a summer day in 1969, Milton Engebretson, the president of the Covenant Church and an enthusiastic flier, invited me to accompany him from Minneapolis to Chicago in a private plane. I have grave reservations about private planes, but on that occasion I agreed to go. By my side in the back seat was my friend Harry Evans, president of Trinity College, in Bannockburn, Illinois.

We left Minneapolis in what seemed good weather, but conditions deteriorated, and when we got to Fox Lake we were caught in a witch's cauldron of black clouds and howling winds.

Our little craft behaved nobly under the skilled hand of my friend Milton, but this did not prevent hair-raising lurches and dizzying falls. I was terrified. I knew existentially what it was to be a feather in a tornado.

In the midst of it, Milton shouted over the roar of the storm, "Are you afraid you're going to die?"

"No," I shouted back. "I'm afraid I'm going to puke."

But despite the terror—the cold sweat and the churning tummy—I was faithful to my game plan. I did not cease to manage. As we plunged earthward or rode madly upward, I planned our funerals. I saw the headlines: "CHURCH LEADERS CRASH IN FLAMES" and the sub-head, "PRIVATE PLANE CARRIES CLERICS TO DEATH." I also arranged the joint funeral service, the honorary pall bearers, the music, the speeches, the flowers. And just before we sneaked out of the last furious vortex of weather, I saw the long solemn lines of black limousines moving into the city of the dead.

Jesus and Our Game Plan

In this context it is helpful to understand Jesus' game plan. His purpose in coming to us was not to give us all the same strategy and the same character. He does not expect us to play the game alike. For many years I felt that being a Christian was being like Jesus and using his game plan. I tried to live like Jesus, serve like Jesus, and suffer like him. There must be millions of people in the world today who are trying to change their game plan to that of our Lord.

But the beautiful thing about the game plan of Jesus is that he came to let us be ourselves. He really doesn't try to make Peter over. He doesn't try to make Paul unlike Paul. He accepts all of the sharp corners and all the strange ways in which people react to existence.

On the other hand, the Lord does not let his game plan be changed. There were many occasions, we may be sure, when Peter tried to convince Jesus that he ought not go ahead with the dreary business of going to Jerusalem and meeting the mass hostility of the Jewish leaders and of the Roman government. But Jesus was unshaken in his resolve. In the same way he resists our efforts today to change his strategy.

Jesus responds to Peter and to us not so much by changing our strategy or altering our character as by monitoring our love for him and finding ways in which our game plan can be fitted in to the larger strategy. I think this means making our game plan serve the ends of relationship, that is, of love.

When Jesus came to Peter and the other disciples on the shore of the lake after the resurrection, Jesus freed Peter to use his own game plan. He said to Peter, "Feed my sheep." In other words, "Take care of my people." It is in this context that Jesus' words to Peter, "You are Peter and on this rock I will build my church" must be seen. Was Peter a rock? Obviously not. He was a cowardly, impulsive, stubborn, take-charge person. He was not a moral or spiritual paragon, but he seems to have been indestructibly himself. And it was on this rock that Jesus was to build his church.

Jesus' game plan is not to make us all alike but to make us ourselves in him. This is the meaning of the phrase in the New Testament about the old Adam and the new Adam. In the presence of Jesus much of the insecurity and the phoniness of the old Adam can be stripped away and in a real sense we can become new people. We can share in the new Adam. But old or new we still remain Adam. Even though we have passed from death into life, the strategy, the game plan, the character remain. Only now the Spirit helps us in the midst of our weakness to use our game plan in loving the brethren.

GROUP DESIGN 4

In groups of three or four, formed at random, or in a more permanent group, answer the following questions:
1. What is my game plan, that is, how do I characteristically respond to a crisis or a longer process of stress? (It is quite possible that you can identify several game plans, more or less related, but for the purpose of the exercise, select the one which is most obvious to you and perhaps to others.)
2. How is God using my game plan to bless other people and even his church?
3. What must I do or have happen to me if my game plan is not to frustrate the larger strategy of our Lord? (For example, Peter may not have changed his game plan of taking over, but he may have found a more effective way of dealing with it.)

5

AM I
A MASK
OR A FACE?

Some years ago I gave a talk to my faculty colleagues on the importance of being professional. I emphasized the difference between faculty and students and deplored what I sensed was, on the part of some teachers, an adolescent over-identification with students.

It was not a bad speech, and it had some truth in it which is still meaningful to me. But I did not then realize that most people in our culture are not too little, but too much, the professional. They live a good part of their lives in their *role* and not in their humanity.

All of us have to find a place to live. We live in a house, of course, and that house is on a street in a town. But actually we live not so much in houses and rooms as in some sort of identity. Our sense of belongingness and comfort, our sense of the rightness of things, our confidence that we can return to something stable in the midst of the uncertainties of our lives depends on where we live—that is, where our existence finds its roots.

Young people talk about being strung out and put together. I suspect that all of us have problems with who we are and that many of us do feel strung out as if our egos were beads on a string. We are not one thing. Rather like the demoniac in the Gospel we are legion.

The problem is complicated for us by our doubleness. We are persons and we are roles. We are professions or trades; we are children, spouses, parents; we are Christians, Jews, atheists; we are mystics or activists; we are intellectuals or Archie Bunkers.

Living in Our Roles

Most of us tend to live in our roles rather than in our humanity because these roles give us a measure of control. And we usually select a role where we are the most competent and hence the most powerful. We like to be our competence. We like to live in our excellence.

Our civilization encourages such competitive role playing. What would a complex society such as ours be like without people aspiring to excellence, polishing their brass, improving their communications skills, working at being a better and better something? We are all engaged in earning brownie points because our society demands it of us. Such points are our credentials. They introduce us to status and power in a community that lives in its roles and in its expertise.

I recently read the statement of the president of a large and prestigious university that has been plagued by student disturbance for the past five years. I was surprised by his rhetoric. It still glistened with terms like "excellence," "intellectual leadership," "educational pioneering," as if all the campus anguish had only been a passing storm and the university was now back on its old course. But then I said to myself, "How inevitable! A university can only live so long as it proves its right to live in the society it serves. It must stress how good it is."

Priestly Medicine

I can recall with a great deal of pain an encounter I had as a fifteen-year-old with an outstanding eye, ear, nose, and throat specialist in our town. He was a man of international reputation and, because I was having serious problems with my tonsils, my parents were anxious to get his help.

I can still remember the morning I was ushered into his brightly lit examining room after having passed through several anterooms—the Court of the Gentiles and the Court of Women—on my way into the Holy of Holies. I am sure that the specialist was a human being, but that morning he functioned as a priest in some esoteric cult. He was himself dressed in a spotless white coat; he was surrounded by starched nurses; and on his head, glittering like a papal mitre, was something I had never seen before but which filled me with terror—a very shiny reflector. I looked to the doctor for some evidence of human sympathy and understanding, but his professional manner was not to smile or to show anything but cold objectivity. He ushered me into an examining chair, asked me to open my mouth, then rammed a formidable stainless-steel instrument into my inflamed throat. He then squeezed the infected tonsils with unbelievable objectivity. As I gagged and squirmed he said to my mother, "The boy is full of pus. The tonsils must be removed at once or he may drop dead at any minute from an infection of the heart." With that he extracted the instrument from my throat and dropped it into a receptacle. After washing his hands he departed brusquely from our presence like a prelate going back to his sacristy.

At no point during that dreary encounter did he let anything of his humanity appear. He did not even show professional sympathy. He seemed to look on suffering from some high unassailable eminence.

I am sure the doctor did not realize that he was actually using his talent, his professional training, and his competence in such a way as to separate himself from people. He may have been a very good-hearted man who, because he could not stand the suffering he was called upon to see day after day, isolated himself in professional armor. But the effect of his expertise on me was to frighten me, to increase my adolescent anxieties, and to make me believe for many years that I was burdened with a bad heart.

Expertise and Isolation

What my internationally renowned surgeon did to me, I subsequently proceeded to do to other people. I became a teacher who taught by terrifying. I am sure that I whipped many a laggard student into response by sarcasm and high-handedness as well as by the challenge to improvement. Unquestionably I was an effective drill sergeant. But I am equally sure that I blasted some flowers in the bud and helped underline the insecurity in those students who did not have enough aggressiveness to fight back.

When I look back on my life, I see myself as an insecure person finding his security in a collection of trophies and merit badges. In high school and college I sought honors paralleling the athletic laurels I could not earn because of innate physical awkwardness. There was hardly a non-curricular or curricular activity—demanding brain not muscle—in which I did not try to excel. Journalism, debate, oratory, music, literature, campus politics, religion, romance—I competed in all of them "to be crowned with a wreath that will not last."

In a way my life's partner was first won as a trophy. When we were in college she was the belle of the campus, and I competed for her as for a loving cup or a ribbon to stick in my coat.

In my mature years I collected board memberships and when possible board chairmanships. Though an avid student of the Bible and of the Apostle Paul, I put my trust in external ceremonies. I was a sort of secular Pharisee living in a succession of meritorious achievements. My expertise was my home, and in many situations people knew me only by my professional pedigree. It is easy for me to identify with the Apostle Paul, when, in his letter to the Philippians he talks about being what he was and now is:

> We do not put any trust in external ceremonies. I could, of course, put my trust in such things. If anyone thinks he can trust in external ceremonies, I have even more reason to feel that way. I was circumcised when I was a week old. I am an Israelite by birth, of the tribe of Benjamin, a pure-blooded Hebrew. So far as keeping the Jewish law is concerned, I was a Pharisee, and I was so zealous that I persecuted the church. So far as a man can be righteous by obeying the commands of the Law, I was without fault. But all those things that I might count as profit I now reckon as loss, for Christ's sake. Not only those things; I reckon everything as complete loss for the sake of what is so much more valuable, the knowledge of Christ Jesus my Lord. For his sake I have thrown everything away, I consider it all as mere garbage, so that I might gain Christ, and be completely united with him (3:3-9 TEV).

73

Plowshares into Swords

What Paul speaks about as characterizing his past I would like to call *spiritual perversion*. It involves beating our talents into weapons of aggression. The prophet Isaiah talks about beating our swords into plowshares and our spears into pruning hooks. But spiritual perversion is reversing the process. People who live in their professional roles beat their plowshares into swords and their pruning hooks into spears. This is the kind of person Paul was before he was converted. He writes, "You have heard what my manner of life was when I was still a practising Jew: how savagely I persecuted the church of God, and tried to destroy it; and how in the practice of our national religion I was outstripping many of my Jewish contemporaries in my boundless devotion to the traditions of my ancestors." (Gal. 1:13-14 NEB). The key word is "outstripping." When we are spiritually perverted, every occasion is an opportunity to compete, to outstrip. We integrate our talents in one ruthless thrust. At whatever cost we have got to be the best. We have got to dominate, to succeed.

I am very much interested in medieval history and I have sometimes tried to place myself imaginatively in that strange world of little kingdoms and principalities, some of them only a few thousand acres in extent. I have wondered what it was like to live in constant fear of being invaded by your neighbors or in the constant hope of doing your neighbor in and becoming his master. What a world of anxiety, vanity, greed, cruelty, bloodshed, and endless feuds!

We flatter ourselves that today we live and let live. It

74

is certainly true that in Western society the outward cruelties have been reduced. But are we right in believing that the inner rivalries are any less bloody? Isn't it true that on university campuses, in the world of business and industry, yes, even within the institutional church itself plowshares are being beaten into swords and pruning hooks into spears?

The effect of this competitive thrust is to negate others. Sometimes we take care of our competitor by a fair criticism of what he presents, but the temptation is to exploit any chink in his armor. In this process almost any weapon will do—innuendos, satire, what the medievals used to call *argumenta ad hominem*, that is, arguments directed not to the matter at hand but to the personal weaknesses of the opponent.

The point in all this is that we not only want to be above others, we want to be unlike them. We want to be special. We want to be unique and frostily excellent.

I have every confidence that a measure of competition is good for all of us. Without such stimulus we may not respond in terms of our capacities. But there is such a thing as a stimulus too much for us, an excellence which destroys us, a superiority so overwhelming and so unfeeling that it freezes us in the hopelessness of our mediocrity.

Such superiority has the effect of destroying not only the humanity of the victim but the humanity of the victor. I shall not soon forget the hurt in the eyes in one of my brothers in the ministry when he summed up years of professionalism on my part in the words, "I always admired you, and I always hated your guts"—which said something about what I had done both to him and to myself.

Conversion to Humanity

From such spiritual perversion we are saved only by conversion to our real humanity. Paul was able to give up the garbage of his superiority and of his professional expertise when he saw in the martyred Stephen the effect of his madness, when in his vision on the road to Damascus he saw that he was in reality persecuting the Lord of glory. And most significantly of all in a street called Straight in Damascus when he was ministered to by a fellow human being who called him "Brother Saul," laid his hands on him, and restored his sight. I think the meaning of this episode is that Christ works through human beings to make us truly human. Paul remained all of his life a person aware of his competence and his credentials. In several of his letters he is careful to point out what a VIP he had once been, and indeed still is and that is honest and OK. But he is also willing to say how much he needs people like Ananias to call him "Brother Saul." In calling Paul "brother" his fellow Christians brought him back to his essential humanness.

My own conversion came about in the same way. In the summer of 1967 I began to see the face of Christ in the face of the people I was criticizing and trying to outstrip and dominate. I understood that what I did to the least of his brothers I was doing to the Lord whom I loved and tried to serve.

I began to see what I had heard talked about for at least 25 years, but had never accepted at gut level, namely that relationships can only be developed at the level of our humanity. God became man in order to relate to us, and man has to become man in order to relate to his brother.

Following that conversion I went through a review of my values. I began to see that the people who had previously threatened me and whom I had categorized as students or professors or radicals or minorities or mere women were in effect human beings to whom I could relate. Many were difficult to deal with. Some were sick. Some had problems with my chemistry. But they were all human beings, and in dealing with them I could leave behind, as the garbage it was, the pretense to expertise and superiority.

I need not tell you that this step forward is a very difficult one to take. To step from competence into humanity—to live in your personhood and your humanness —is a kind of dying. To be able to confess that you have the same needs, weaknesses, and sins as every other human being asks something of you which is almost impossible to give.

We recall the story of the minister and his associate who came into their empty sanctuary one morning and knelt on the altar steps and audibly confessed their sinfulness and unworthiness. When they had finished, they heard the voice of the custodian from the back of the church, "O Lord, forgive *my* sin and unworthiness." And the minister turned to his associate and said, "Look who thinks he is unworthy." Even in our confession we like to think of ourselves as special.

The step from expertise into humanity is impossible without the example and energy of Jesus and his sacrifice. Because he who was equal with God became a man out of love for us and died the death of a common criminal, it is possible for us to die the death he died.

I would like to make one final point. To live in our

humanity does not mean that we are to deny our talents and develop a dishonest humility. Our talents and their development through training and experience may, through the chemistry of grace, become gifts. The difference between using and abusing, perverting and converting our abilities lies in how we look at them. If we see our talents primarily as means to control and manipulate others, they become weapons in our hands; we turn our plowshares into swords. But if we see them as gifts from God, which he both gives and takes away in the beautiful impermanence of our time on earth, we'll use them as plowshares and pruning hooks—gifts to gladden ourselves and others. We shall then, in Bacon's happy phrase, be using our talents to the glory of God and the relief of man's estate.

GROUP DESIGN 5

Share the following questions with one other person. You may want to do this on a walk that allows enough time for a frank interchange (both speaking and listening) or in some other leisurely setting:

1. In what particular role which I am called on to play (parent, husband, wife, employee, neighbor, churchman, or woman) is it easiest for me to be a real person?

2. In which role is it most difficult?

3. What is the connection between the role, or roles, I must play and the particular gifts I feel I have been given?

6

A PLANE
MADE
TO FLY

Contemporary psychologists disagree on the deepest human crisis. Some, like Freud, associate it with sexual feelings toward parent figures. Others think of it as the trauma associated with birth. Still others talk about the terror of nothingness or the anxiety of not-OK-ness.

In the Bible the major human crisis seems to be the experience of being cut off from God and the faith community, and the two are not always easy to distinguish.

Psychologists see a diversity of ways in which human beings handle their awesome crises. In the Bible contact with God is restored not by some human act but by a human cry, that is, by prayer. In Psalm 116:1-9 (NEB) we read:

> I love the Lord, for he has heard me
> and listens to my prayer;
> for he has given me a hearing
> whenever I have cried to him.
> The cords of death bound me,
> Sheol held me in its grip.
> Anguish and torment held me fast;
> so I invoked the Lord by name,
> 'Deliver me, O Lord, I beseech thee;
> for I am thy slave.'

Gracious is the Lord and righteous,
  our God is full of compassion.
The Lord preserves the simple-hearted;
  I was brought low and he saved me.
Be at rest once more, my heart,
  for the Lord has showered gifts upon you.
He has rescued me from death
  and my feet from stumbling.
I will walk in the presence of the Lord
  in the land of the living.

The RSV renders verse 8 with rather more feeling:

For thou hast delivered my soul from death, my
eyes from tears, my feet from stumbling.

Despite the centrality of biblical faith in the fashioning of our Western culture many of us have been taught to respond to fear not so much by prayer as by decisive action. C. S. Lewis talks about the persistence in Christian thought of the *bellum intestinum*—the internal war—in which moral courage is seen as triumphing over unbelievable odds. Responding to fear by trying harder is so much a part of our daily life that we carry it with us into business competition, into our struggle with our studies, and certainly into the arena of athletic competition. The motto of the Avis Company, "We try harder," is the most common way in which we deal with fear.

Made to Fly

There is nothing particularly wrong with this as a way of life—if we understand its very real limits. Some years ago when I was still overcoming my repugnance to flying, a repugnance which still remains, a friend of mine who has a private plane for business purposes offered to fly me from a town in the San Joaquin Valley to San Francisco. Knowing of my fear in a plane he suggested that once we were airborne I try to fly his single-engine plane. I believe it was his conviction that if I could feel the plane flying, I might overcome my fear of the air. And so when we were at an altitude of about 8000 feet and moving northward across a mountain range, he gave me the plane to fly. As soon as I had hold of the stick, one dominant emotion began to control me. It was to keep the nose of the plane headed up. I had an instinctive feeling, which I'm sure was irrational that if I could keep the plane pointing up, it would not come down. Unfortunately I was so determined in the direction I wanted to fly that fairly soon the plane began to climb almost vertically. My friend and pilot laughed, resumed control of the airplane and we were soon back on even course. It was then he said to me, "They all do it; they all pull back on the stick when they're scared." Then a little later, "Why don't you relax in this airplane? It was made to fly. This plane wants to fly. Why don't you let it?"

I believe that God has designed us to fly and not to crash. In spite of that, our lives are lived in response to fear. I find myself tense, and I begin pulling back on the stick. I am not at all sure that President Roosevelt was right when in 1933 he told the American people, "We have nothing to fear but fear itself." There are many things that pose an objective threat to us and that we have a legitimate right to fear. Our existence is difficult. It is threatened by many hazards: ill health, unemployment, the tragic death of our loved ones, social miseries of the worst kind, and international catastrophes far beyond our power to control.

So it is not my purpose to argue against the existence of objective fear. Instead I want to talk about the way we handle our fears. The Apostle Paul often dealt with his fears by asserting his right to be in control. His letter to the Galatians is an interesting example of how he handles the panic he feels in the face of an adulteration of his gospel and a challenge to his apostolic authority. To overcome his fear, he emphasizes his case of independence from the Christian fellowship and claims in strong language that his right to be an apostle came directly from the Lord himself.

Too Much Control

All my life I have been doing the same thing. I was no more than two-and-a-half years old and living in southern Sweden with my mother and two sisters and a brother when I began to assume control. At that time my father was absent from the family. His business commitments carried him into Czarist Russia, and he was gone for several months at a time. During these days of loneliness for my mother I asserted my responsibility for her by parading back and forth on the rag runner which covered our floor and proclaiming that I would be her "little daddy," that as far as I was concerned my father did not need to return from Russia because I would take care of my mother. The Freudian implications of this boast are obvious, but not entirely germane to my point, which is that we begin early to crawl into the driver's seat.

But the same way of handling my fear returned at the age of seven when my mother was forced to leave me in a provincial hospital for ten days while she returned to take care of the other children. I was full of infection and fear, but I still remember choosing not to use the stretcher which was wheeled up to take me to surgery, and walking down the corridors myself. I even insisted on climbing up on the operating table. I would probably have walked back to my bed if I had not been under anesthesia.

Years later when I assumed the presidency of a college, which was not only relatively small but poor and untried besides, I asked in my inaugural address, not for a large school, but a great one. I had the stick pulled way back.

Thus my life has run its course. I have really been dominated by two fears—two terrors. Because I was unblessed, I was afraid of too much success. I felt I did not deserve it. But I was also dominated by the fear of failure. My whole life has been characterized by a tense pulling back on the stick, keeping the nose of the airplane headed so far into the clouds that at any moment I was in danger of performing an Immelmann turn.

The Inadequate Man

Then a few years ago I discovered, through some very beautiful people, that pulling back on the stick was not going to save me. This proved to be a fantastic revelation to me. The realization that I did not have to be adequate for myself and for everybody else and in all situations; the realization that all of the people around me who seemed cool and competent were as frightened as I was; the realization that in the face of the complexity and difficulty of life, the wisest and most virtuous of us is indeed inadequate—was like a new birth for me.

83

I began to understand what it meant to trust God and to fly the airplane he had designed for me. I did not have to flap my wings or trample the air. I just had to accept what I was and live within the limits of my mortality. I began to understand at the feeling level what Isaiah means when he says, "Do you not know, have you not heard? The Lord, the everlasting God, creator of the wide world, grows neither weary nor faint; no man can fathom his understanding. He gives vigour to the weary, new strength to the exhausted. Young men may grow weary and faint, even in their prime they may stumble and fall; but those who look to the Lord will win new strength, they will grow wings like eagles; they will run and not be weary, they will march on and never grow faint" (Isa. 40:23-31 NEB).

Out of this new relaxation and self-acceptance, there came the slow assurance that it was OK to be me and that no one had the right to hook me in my guilt feelings or to design my life for me. If I no longer needed to pull back on the stick because of the OK-ness of grace, neither was I obligated to respond to the sickness in other people —to yield passively to their manipulations. Letting the plane God has given me fly itself also made me feel OK about being human and not some sort of demagogue. I no longer needed to be involved in the process of denying my humanity. I was a person filled with the chaos of feelings—rage, greed, lust, ambition, envy, even malice. Instead of repressing these feelings and proclaiming myself superhuman, I could now admit to them and pray for the health to deal with them constructively and positively. Finally my new stance permitted me to accept the fact that I needed people and their ministry. I was no longer the adequate man, showering my blessings on people from above. I was a person desperately in need of the ministry other people could bring me.

One-Engine Plane

Having said this, I do not want to leave the impression that things are better than they are. The plane I fly is not an indestructible projectile, but a little one-engine plane buffeted by mountain winds and threatened by every form of natural force. Though the plane was not designed to crash, I'm aware of the fact that it may crash. Before I land my plane for the last time, a variety of circumstances will test my courage. But now, because I must not assume full responsibility for everything I do and for everything other people do, even failure is beginning to seem less threatening to me. I do not yet have the freedom to fail. I still keep pulling back on the stick to be perfectly secure. But I'm beginning to understand what freedom to fail means. And I'm beginning to understand what Paul means when he says that God has made us more than conquerors through him who loved us. Whether we fail or succeed, we belong to him and, in a way impossible before, we belong to ourselves.

GROUP DESIGN 6

In a group of three or four share the answers to the following questions:

1. In what one area of my life do I feel secure enough to perform without pressing, that is without being dominated by the fear of failure? (For example, athletics,

cooking, decorating my home, sailing, gardening, disciplining our children, speaking publicly, chairing a meeting, making a sale, buying clothes, counseling someone in trouble, visiting a sick person, explaining the meaning of a Bible passage, taking an examination, conferring with my employer, conferring with an employee, etc.) What is the source of my security: talent, training, experience, personal charm, or charisma?

2. In what specific area am I dominated by the fear of failure to the point where not even common sense or careful reasoning prevent my "pulling back on the stick"? (For example, any of the above or other situations such as facing surgery, going to the dentist, public witnessing, trying to sell something, managing or administering a project, serving as an instructor, confronting my parents, dealing with my spouse or children, encountering my pastor, communicating bad news, announcing a new regulation, or a difficult, unpopular project which must be carried through?)

3. What strategy and resources do I see as available to me in the second of these situations?

7

MUCH WINE
AND
LITTLE

According to John (2:1-11), Jesus' first miracle was at Cana where at a wedding feast he turned 130 gallons of water into wine. People in my tradition have difficulty associating Jesus with wine even in small quantities, but 500 quarts of it seem a little much. A friend of mine reports the reaction of a parishioner, a woman whom he was seeking to convince of Jesus' latitude in the matter of wine drinking. She said, "That's the one thing I don't like about Jesus. I don't like that he drank wine." Which suggests that she was more devoted to the demands of abstinence than to the person of her Lord.

Much Wine

Be that as it may, two things are important about the miracle: that water was changed into wine and that there was an abundance of the latter. Hence the inner meaning of the miracle is that God stands ready to transform the ordinary meaningless, and even painful, events of our life into happenings, crammed with gladness and that he will do this in such a way as to overwhelm us with his generosity. Aldous Huxley talks about the ducal quality in Jesus. The impression our Lord creates in this miracle is of largesse—a magnanimous, flowing, illimitable open-handedness.

Recently I went to church and heard David Luecke, my minister, talk about water changed into wine, and I really believed in that moment that God stands ready to surprise us with his abundance and to bring life out of death.

But the next day I accompanied my wife Sally to the hospital for major surgery, and my faith, so splendid in the sanctuary, began to wither. By Tuesday when her operation was scheduled, my confidence had been reduced to something near zero. Two things were getting to me: the surgery itself and the fear that the surgery might reveal something inoperable. I no longer expected the eighteen firkins of wine in the Cana miracle. I don't know what I expected. I know that my mouth was dry, my palms sweaty, and my stomach tied in knots.

After the nurse had come in to administer a sedative and had rolled Sally into the elevator, I went into the visitors' lounge. I tried to convince myself that as a Christian, I had nothing to fear. But the fact was that I was afraid. The hollowness inside me was so painful that I wanted to roll into a ball and sneak into the darkest corner available. Emotionally I was assuming the fetal position and physically I was hunched over and staring at my shoes.

At that moment the head nurse came in and suggested that I go to lunch so that I would be available when the doctor returned from surgery. I looked at her with dull eyes. "Lunch? What's that?" I said to myself. I didn't want to eat. I didn't want to breathe. The great desperate passages from Elijah, Job, and the Psalms came to me. It was a kind of interior suicide which continued as I followed the endless corridors of the hospital toward the cafeteria.

Strangely enough the story of the Cana miracle went with me. I thought about sorrow being turned into joy, and I believed in the God who can bring such miracles about. What I did not believe was that such a miracle could happen to me at that moment. I did not believe that there was any wine for me at all.

A Little Wine

I picked up a ham and cheese sandwich in the cafeteria line and a square of cranberry jello salad and a piece of pecan pie and a coke. And as I placed these mundane things on the tray and began to move toward the cashier line, I thought of something else from the life of Jesus—an episode from the very end. He was on the cross in his final moments of agony, and he groaned to those standing around or perhaps to himself, "I am thirsty." And, the story continues: "A bowl was there, full of cheap wine; they soaked a sponge in the wine . . . and lifted it up to his lips. Jesus took the wine and said, 'It is finished!' "

It was then I began to pray, not for the 18 firkins of party wine but for a little bit, perhaps what could be picked up by a sponge. I asked for enough joy to carry me through the next hour.

I circled around the crowded cafeteria looking for a place to sit. Irrationally I prayed for a known face. But hospital cafeterias at the lunch hour are busy and preoccupied with nurses and doctors and orderlies carrying on their own "in" conversations. The only vacant place which did not put me in the role of an intruder was across from a young black. I asked if it would be OK to sit down, and he flashed me a shy but warm smile.

He was Teience Lavette Green of Baltimore. He was being admitted to the hospital for the removal of a kidney, damaged when a car crashed into his bicycle a year ago. I asked him how he felt. He told me he was scared even though he knew he was in a great hospital and in the hands of the best surgeons. He wanted to be a professional basketball player, and everything hinged on how the operation would go.

It was then I could tell him how anxious I was because a person very important to me was in surgery. He listened as only people slowed down by their own pain can listen, and his listening helped me. It was as if my tongue parched by my fear had been touched ever so fleetingly by a sponge soaked in wine. It was not a big, dizzying joy, but it was enough joy to let me survive.

Inching Along

Sometimes we live by soaring and sometimes by inching along through doubts, anxieties, failures. I believe that God has a little bit of wine for us in our worst moments, and he used a frightened and lonely sixteen year old to tell me that.

Jesus drank his sip of sour wine and bowed his head and died. And on the other side a million angels readied their trumpets to awaken him to the new gladness. That's all there too: not only weakness and shame lived through, but incredible glory—firkins, and barrels, and lakes of

90

wedding wine, the best saved until the last. But we probably do not understand that great culminating miracle as we should until in the moment of pain or loss he has touched our lips with a little wine, no more than is held in a sponge.

GROUP DESIGN 7

Share with one other person your response to the following questions:

1. In what specific situation have I experienced water being changed into wine? That is, boring, painful, scary, or even tragic circumstances have been transformed in such a way that in them God has revealed himself to me?

2. At this moment what particular thing is causing me pain, grief, or anxiety? What, if any, hope do I have that the water may be changed to wine and the glory of the Lord revealed?

3. What means do I see God using to transform my trying experience and that of others into a good, that is, to turn water into wine?

8

OIL
OF
GLADNESS

Since I was very small I have had problems with the doctrine of the "last things." That things should end in particular deaths seemed bad enough, but that they should end in a general bang seemed not only frightening but mad. I really liked the earth too much to see it go up in smoke, and the prospect of the moon turning to blood and the stars falling was the final dreariness.

I have since revised my ideas about an *eschaton*. I now realize that everything is renewed by death and resurrection, and a manifestation of God's tough love for us is the fact of the Last Judgment. Especially is this so if we see judgment as *restoration* rather than as condemnation. Jesus' word in John 3:17 is helpful: "For God did not send his Son into the world to be its Judge, but to be its Savior" (TEV).

One of the aspects of the "last things" that struck me where I hurt was the need of being ready for the unexpected. The warning that the Day would come as "a thief in the night" turned me into jelly. An especially painful form of that warning was the parable of the ten virgins. This frightening story with its concluding, "Watch out," seemed to preach preparedness, foresight, prudence—virtues I had in short supply.

Let us look at the action of the parable in Matthew 25:1-13. An oriental bridegroom is escorted to the bride's house by a following of unmarried girls—the number determined by the status and resources of the bridegroom's family. The wedding procession is held at night; the lamps serve both to light the path of the bridegroom into the house and to heighten the feeling of festivity.

The escort in our story is formed by five girls who have oil both in their lamps and in their "backup tanks" and five others who, although they have oil in their lamps, have nothing in reserve. The task of escorting the bridegroom and lighting the wedding chamber is the basis for including the girls in the celebration in the first place. Hence when the five girls who run out of oil can no longer perform their prime function, they are shut out from the party.

On the surface, and certainly in the preaching of most clergymen, when I was a child, the contrast between the wise and the foolish girls was quite simple. One group was ready, the other was not. The wise girls had made provision for their future. They were the solid citizens—the methodical girls who were active in the Girl Scouts, gave out the pencils in the classroom, and cleaned the board and erasers at the end of the day. They were the teacher's helpers who wrote neatly on the board, enunciated each word they spoke, composed grammatically, and faced the future with assurance.

The foolish girls? Well, they were like me. They were never prepared for anything. I remember the terror inspired in me by my brother's second class Scout badge, a brass ribbon on which were inscribed the words "Be pre-pared." And I still tremble when Delta Airlines announces cheerfully that "Delta is ready when you are." Dear hearts at Delta, I am never ready.

It started very early. But it climaxed my first day in the little country school in the family's home parish in southern Sweden. I was younger than my classmates and frightened by the novelty of the situation and by the need to be adequate. In the mid-morning recess with the schoolyard full of strange and boisterous children, I made my way to the area where I assumed the school toilets to be. Typically I had not inquired which one was the boys' and which the girls'. I turned the corner, saw the door of a toilet half-open, darted in and seated myself on one of the eight holes made available. Before long the door was pulled open and three or four blonde pinafore-clad girls, all older than I, started into the room. When they saw me, they let out a howl of derisive laughter. I can still see red convulsed faces at the toilet door. The first day in school I commit the unbelievable gaff of entering the girls' toilet. I can hear the laughter. I am caught literally with my pants down. I am not ready.

Time would fail me if I were to recount all the painfully embarrassing moments from my childhood which supported my conviction that I was among the foolish. When other children opened their neat lunch packages—sandwiches there, cookies there, fruit there, a bottle of milk—I fumbled into my paper bag which I had dropped a few times en route, or sat on or stepped on, to find my sandwiches mashed, my apple covered with butter, and my cookie (when it was available) in crumbs. I was never neat, orderly, adequate.

The same kind of red-faced embarrassment has followed me through life. At college term papers were typed out the last moment, exams prepared in the gray dawn of the day of wrath, daily assignments gulped down with the morning coffee. I was never ready.

I spent five years in the army, trembling at the notice, "Prepare for inspection." I dreaded the missing button, the unpressed trouser crease, the cloudy brass. But I never improved. I saw my fellow officers lug piles of soiled laundry and clothing to the cleaners to be ready for the judgment, but I had nothing in reserve. I saw them patiently at work on shoes and belt buckles and brass buttons, but I did not join them early enough in their laborious preparedness. I came to the day of inspection with a dry mouth and wet hands. I was never ready.

If the parable means what at one level it seems to mean, I'll never make it. It is true that I have learned, out of motives of insecurity and fear of public humiliation, to make peace with most of the demands of the community. I do get my bills paid, my grass cut, and most of my work finished. But I never enjoy the feeling of having anticipated a dead-line: the manuscript neatly typed and boxed; the correspondence answered; all "the harvest gathered in ere the winter storms begin."

So if the parable means that the imprudent are out, then I am out. I'll never join the solid girls marching into the wedding chamber, their pleased eyes swiveling right and left.

But the parable also has a more direct application. To be foolish meant being caught in the wrong place or in the wrong activity when Jesus came. My first visit to a theater at the age of nine was disturbed by the rumble of a passing freight train. Even though I was in the place with my parents' permission, I visualized the ceiling splitting open and the terrible glory of the Rapture revealed. I became convinced early that I did not want to hear the last trumpet in an amusement park, pool hall, or movie palace.

As I grew older, being ready for Jesus came to mean being active in the Lord's work rather than "fleeting the time as they did in the golden world." This meant reading the Bible systematically, praying, witnessing, giving, serving (mostly in unpleasant situations), attending church meetings, and suffering. I once heard a minister say that he would like to meet the Lord when he was preaching about the Second Coming—which, I suppose, meant that he then considered himself at his best.

Coupled with this list of recommended activities was a negative one, the burden of which was that in view of the impending *parousia,* Christians should maintain decorum in their day-to-day life. Times of hilarity or bursts of self-indulgence were not thought a proper atmosphere in which to meet the Lord of glory. What this adds up to is a widely held conviction that the only valid form of readiness is piety.

I can no longer believe that. By that standard the pharisees would be "readier" than the publicans, and the scribes would outrun the prostitutes into the wedding chamber.

To Be Ready Is to Make Joy a Habit

I don't believe the parable is talking about the relative readiness of good and bad, prudent and imprudent people, if by readiness we mean control or coping in the ordinary sense. Life and death are too big for that kind of managing. Who is equal to these things?

I think the parable is talking about joy. The heart of the story is a wedding. For our Lord the party and the wedding were central. In these occasions of festivity the joy and freedom of grace arise from relationships. The wedding is the glad union of all creation with its creator— the morning stars singing together—and it is the happy union of two people in the full dimensions of their existence, and it is the joyous fashioning into one body of all the members, disparate and perhaps somewhat reluctant, of the body of Christ.

Jesus invites us to joy. He invites us to enter into the "joy of the Lord." He encourages us to push through to the burning gladness at the center of human experience. Hebrews 12:2 refers to Jesus "who for the joy that was set before him endured the cross." (TEV renders it, "He did not give up because of the cross! On the contrary, because of the joy that was waiting for him, he thought nothing of the disgrace of dying on the cross.")

To have oil in our lamp means to have joy with us as fact and promise. It does not mean to call sorrow joy, as if the sorrow could be ignored. It does not mean making the best of a bad situation in the manner of Polyanna.

To Be Ready Is Finding Joy in Relationships

Oil in our lamps means to have joy in the midst of problems because we are in relationship with God and with other people. As I write this I am torn with anxiety about Katherine, our infant granddaughter who may not make it. We don't know at this moment, but we live in shadows. We are tempted to let the oil burn out and to let the darkness take over. To be foolish. Which means to withdraw into isolation. To refuse to seek God and one another in this experience. To believe that because the Bridegroom tarries, he does not exist and he will not come. To believe in death but not in resurrection.

We are tempted to be foolish, but the Holy Spirit gives us another option—to be wise. To be wise is not to run away from grief. God forbid. On the other hand, it is not to seek it. I have a right to pray that the cup will pass. I have a right to pray that the infant Katherine will be the beautiful person she promises to be.

Job has the right to rail at God, to question him, to challenge him to come out from his silence so that he can argue with him (Job 23). The psalmist has a right to groan and hold his head and ask why God has forsaken him (Psalm 22). Paul has a right to "give up all hope of living" and to feel that "the sentence of death" has been passed on him. (2 Cor. 1:8-9). Is not this what our Lord is teaching us in his prayer in the garden, "My father if it is possible, take this cup away from me!" (In other words, "I don't want this thing to happen to me"). But not what I want, but what you want." And a little later, "My Father, if this cup cannot be taken away unless I drink it, your will be done" (Matthew 26:39, 42 TEV).

To Be Ready Is to Wait for the Great Joy

Wisdom, then, is not so much to let grief and anguish go unchallenged as it is to wait for something else in the midst of it. To be wise is to believe that the Spirit will come to help us, weak as we are. It is to know that we do not know how to pray, but to believe that the Spirit pleads with God for us in groans that words cannot express (God praying with himself). To be wise is seeing in an impossible vision the Spirit pleading with God on behalf of his people and in accordance with his will (Romans 8). To be wise is to believe, despite all evidence to the contrary, that nothing can separate us from his love.

To be wise is to have the joy which makes us ready for joy. A friend tells me that after a crushing experience in her marriage, she gave up on joy. She slammed the door in its face. She would lie in bed in the morning and watch decay take over: dust gathering on furniture and carpets, grime clouding the windows, a damp untidiness invading the bedclothes. She lay staring at nothing while the ashtrays overflowed and the unwashed coffee cups accumulated.

Then one day she said, "I want joy back, but it will not come so long as my house and I are so unexpecting. I must will to believe that in spite of everything, joy is at the door. And I shall prepare myself for joy by acting as if it were here. What I think this means," she said, "is that I will no longer believe that I deserve only pain. I will not continue to nourish a sick guilt and invite the darkness."

"I shall clean my house, wash my dishes, empty my ashtrays, launder my clothes, get my hair fixed, buy a new dress. Joy may not come today but if I am ready, there is a sense in which it is already here. If I do not prepare, joy will have ceased to exist for me."

This, I think, is what C. S. Lewis is saying in *The*

Great Divorce. We do not create heaven or hell, but we prepare ourselves for both by what we carry within us day after day. To yield only to despair, to buy nothing but darkness at the store, is to prepare ourselves for outer night where no stars sing. But to buy all the oil we can carry, to peer through the darkness for the tarrying bridegroom, to weep and groan and rejoice at once, to stand on tiptoe in expectation of the morning until our feet get tired, and in the midst of it to nurse the tender flame of gladness—this is to be ready and to enter in.

He comes who will come and does not tarry. To have oil in our lamp is to be surprised and overwhelmed by the *eschaton*—the beautiful Last Thing—but it is also to be at home with it, the way, when having followed a creek through many bends, we find it dizzyingly right that it should join the sea.

GROUP DESIGN 8

Share with two or three others the following questions. It is assumed that a level of trust has been created in the group.

1. What particular event or circumstance in my life at this moment finds me unprepared or unable to cope?

2. What specific change in the situation would I be ready to pray for?

3. If the change I desire does not come about, what resources are available to me for dealing with the situation?

CREATING YOUR OWN RELATIONAL BIBLE STUDIES

At some point after introducing the group to the concept and method of relational Bible study, the leader may want to give the members a chance to develop their own studies.

He will find it helpful to introduce this session by a clarifying discussion of the four principles presented in Chapter 2: *Make the passage my story. Identify with a character. Find the gospel for me. Give the story a name.* When he is certain that the principles are understood, he may want to use the following procedure.

In groups of three, formed at random, each participant is asked to select his favorite story or passage from the Bible and to prepare a brief relational Bible study, using the four principles developed in Chapter 2. The entire group may be told earlier that this is the planned design so that they can spend some time thinking about what they want to share, or 20 to 30 minutes may be given for individual study on the spot.

When the groups of three are assembled, each member of the group is given six minutes to present his relational Bible study, applying the four principles introduced above. When the first participant has finished, the other two members of the group are given a chance to respond with questions or comments.

Following this exchange, the second member of the group is given six minutes for his Bible study, and this is followed by another five minutes of response.

When all three members of the groups have presented their studies and time has been given for response to each study, all the groups may be called together for a debriefing, with opportunity given for feedback.

When the relational, personal emphasis is kept in these studies, there is little opportunity for moralizing or preaching or for sliding past the pain of the issues by stereotypes such as, "The Bible is the answer" or "Jesus never fails." There is also little room for merely restating experiences of the past which no longer have a cutting edge.

GUIDELINES FOR TEN RELATIONAL BIBLE STUDIES

COVER-UP

Scriptural Content: Genesis 3:7-13

Sin is transgression of a command, but it is also concealment of what we have done. We are guilty and we feel ashamed. We are afraid to be discovered, and we try to conceal our nakedness with some hurry-up defense. Sin is inventive. "They sewed fig-leaves together and made themselves aprons." The transgression and the hiding lead to a broken relationship with God and with other people. The final step is blaming. Adam blames Eve who blames the serpent.

Out of transgression, shame, fear, concealment, broken relationships, and projection of guilt on others, come enmity, pain, cursing, thorns and thistles, and a cruel and meaningless life.

The way back to relationship with God and others has been provided by God in Jesus. Because of Jesus, we dare admit who we are and what we do and how we feel. We dare be open with one another. "If we confess . . . he is faithful and just to forgive . . . and to cleanse" (John 1:9).

And "if we live in the light just as he is in the light, we have fellowship with one another."

Application

During the Senate investigation of Watergate the word "cover-up" was used frequently.

In one way or another we are all guilty of "cover-up." The question is not if our cover-up is big and dramatic and has an effect on the nation, but if it has an effect on us. For example, a pastor once confessed to me that he stole sermons and never developed his own. The effect on him was a drying up of creativity and a sense of producing nothing but "thorns and thistles."

The gospel is not that we need to confess to everybody but that we need to confess to somebody. We need to tell someone "This is the way it is for me." Sometimes the "someone" is the person or persons we have wronged; sometimes it is not. Indiscriminate confession often meets only our own neurotic needs, and absolute openness can be destructive. But in spite of these hazards, all of us need to pray for more openness and less cover-up.

And the gospel is, "If we confess, he will forgive and cleanse."

Questions for Twos

1. What one thing am I "covering-up" which I need to deal with? (It is important in this connection to stress that we are not dealing primarily with lurid sins or dramatic concealments, but with dumb, ordinary things. For example, I may be "covering up" my gratitude for a trait or an action of a member of my family, or I may be sitting on a positive feeling in relation to someone.)

2. What is the "cover-up" doing to my relationships?

3. How can I best deal with this situation?

GOD'S NAME: I'LL BE AROUND

Scriptural Content: Exodus 3:1-15

In this passage God calls Moses by name and when Moses asks God for his name, God tells him, it is YHWH, "I Am Who I Am."

A Jewish friend translates this, "I am he who will be around." Or "I'll be around." In other words, God is a God of action, of promise and hope.

Notice all the active words, "I have *seen*," "I have *heard*," "I *know*," "I have *come down* to *deliver* and to *bring them up* out of that land to a good and broad land, a land flowing with milk and honey."

What is significant in this story is the balance of identities. God's identity is important but so is Moses'. Beyond that, the identity of one establishes the identity of the other. When Moses asks God, "Who am I that I should go to Pharaoh?," God answers, "But I will be with you" (3:11-12). In other words, Moses can be Moses because God is with him. But, strangely, God also becomes known and establishes his identity by reference to people.

"Say this to the people of Israel, the Lord, the God of your Fathers, the God of Abraham, the God of Isaac, the God of Jacob, has sent me to you: this is my name forever, and thus I am to be remembered throughout all generations."

Furthermore, Moses becomes Moses in a decisive action: appearing before Pharaoh.

Application

The behavioral sciences are dealing with the importance of personal identity and authenticity as well as with the need of self-acceptance. "I'm OK, you're OK."

This is an important truth in both secular and religious

circles. But the Christian faith adds an important dimension. My identity is established and sustained by God's identity. He guarantees my uniqueness.

Beyond that, my growth in authentic personhood helps to clarify and establish God's identity. This is what it means to glorify God. When I am OK, God's name is made great.

There is another beautiful truth. I become me when I dare to act authentically and decisively. In that situation God "will be around" both to establish me and to reveal himself.

Questions for Fours

1. What is my name? In other words, who am I? (It may be valuable here to have the participant state his name and try to explain how he got that name and what it means to him.)

2. How does God's name ("I'll be around") help to make my name more meaningful to me?

3. What one decisive action do I have to take which, because God is in it with me, may glorify his name?

CRIPPLED AT THE KING'S TABLE

Scriptural Content: 2 Samuel 9:1-13

After the death of Saul and Jonathan in a battle with the Philistines at Mount Gilboa, David assumed the throne of Israel. After he had "settled in," he raised the question of our story, "Is there still anyone left of the house of Saul, that I may show him kindness for Jonathan's sake?"

There was one surviving son of Jonathan, Mephibosheth, a cripple. The story of Mephibosheth is told in 2 Sam. 4:4. He was a boy of five when the bad news came from Mt. Gilboa. His nurse picked him up and in the haste to flee the palace, dropped him, crippling his feet.

David made room for Mephibosheth in his palace, despite the prince's protest, "What is your servant, that you should look upon a dead dog such as I?" The sick and the crippled may have been shown a compassion in Israel which they were not accorded elsewhere, but they weren't treated in a very kingly manner.

But, the story tells us, Mephibosheth "ate always at the king's table" and "was lame in both his feet."

Application

The Christian faith proclaims the miracle of healing, and we are encouraged to press toward health and wholeness, even though wholeness is not a condition for acceptance by God or the community of love.

Despite our healthy concern for being made whole, all of us carry about with us various kinds of lameness which will probably stay with us as long as we live. "The church," said Kierkegaard, "is a hospital." In one sense we may call it a hospital for incurables. In this life no one will be perfected, no matter how eager or persevering.

That is the point with our story. The gospel is that we may eat at the King's table even though we are lame in both our feet.

I feel the truth of this as I get older. There were weaknesses I thought I would outgrow, stupidities I thought I could transcend. But I remain a cripple.

Yet, miracle of miracles, God accepts me, and his loving family accepts me. They may get impatient with my stumbling feet, my self-pity, and my rationalizations; they may pray sternly for my healing. But when the table is set, there is always a place for me.

There used to be an interpretation of this text which made Jonathan a Jesus figure. Mephibosheth was shown kindness for Jonathan's sake; we are accepted because of Jesus. That's an acceptable interpretation for me. I don't think I could tolerate the burning charity of God without the mediation of Jesus. He makes it OK to dangle my crippled feet under the King's table. Because of him I do not fear love that is so awesome and so kingly.

Questions for Fours

1. In my search for wholeness, what particular weakness do I see myself dealing with effectively?

2. What "lameness" do I have which doesn't seem to yield to change or healing?

3. How do I feel about submitting this "lameness" honestly to a group of caring people?

DEATH AND LIFE IN THE AFTERNOON

Scriptural Content: 2 Samuel 11-12

The story of David and Bathsheba is great literature but it is also good psychology and theology. The key to the passage is found in the very first verse: "In the spring of the year, the time when kings go forth to battle, David sent Joab [against the Ammonites] . . . but David remained at Jerusalem."

The warrior king is back from a great victory over the Syrians. When the spring comes and a new war looms on the horizon, David stays at home. He may have been guilty, he may have been anxious, he may have been bored. But whatever the state of his mind, he assumed that he had the resources to set things straight.

He saw a woman who "turned him on," and in spite of the law of God against adultery and the law of comradeship against cheating on your friends, David used his power to steal Bathsheba from her husband. And then he compounded the felony by having the husband "rubbed out" in battle.

So that in a chain of events starting innocently on a spring afternoon David broke at least six of the commandments:

1. He dishonored God.

2. He coveted his neighbor's wife.

3. He bore false witness in the sense that he suppressed the truth.

4. He stole.

5. He committed adultery.

6. He murdered.

The beautiful thing about David when he was confronted

by Nathan the prophet was that he made no defense. He said quite simply to the prophet, "I have sinned against the Lord."

Application

This passage is not a sermon against leisure or reasonable rest or the delegation of authority or even against sex. It is a helpful fluoroscopic view of how power works in all of us.

At no time do we need to be so sensitive to our humanity as when we have achieved an important goal. At that moment we may, like Eve in Milton's Paradise, feel "divinity within us breeding wings." Blood flows fully within us, our muscles are toned up, our eyes are clear, our mind razor sharp. And then "poof!" we fall flat on our face. Before we know it and in our wild scramble to get back into balance, we complicate and complicate. Our spring afternoon turns into a nightmare.

What we need to remember is not that Christians, if they are careful, can avoid these traps, but that even after we have goofed, or sinned, the Lord hears us. The Christian is not asked to be a paragon of every virtue, he is only asked to admit before the Lord and other people where he is.

Questions for Twos

1. On a line opposite poles of success and failure, where are you right now and how do you feel about it? Elated, depressed, confused, anxious, guilty, bitter?

2. Who is the Nathan in your life who helps you to get your bearings and who communicates the gospel?

3. What is the grace you are hoping for in this situation and how may it look to you?

A MAN FOR ANY SEASON

Scriptural Content: 2 Samuel 23:20

"And Benaiah, the son of Jehoiada, was a valiant man. . . . He went down and slew a lion in a pit on a day when snow had fallen."

We know little more about Benaiah than that he was one of David's "mighty men"—a member of the royal bodyguard. And we have the brief account of the occasion when, on whatever pretext or challenge or command, he performed this feat of strength.

The text tells us that the thing was done

1. at a bad time (snow)

2. in an inconvenient place (a pit)

3. to a most formidable opponent (a lion).

Application

Most of us are not crisis-seekers; we do not normally look for trouble. But trouble comes to all of us or to people we care for, and we may be called on to confront a difficult situation or person. The trouble may be personal, involving only us and our family, or it may be communal and social.

In this situation it may be right to develop a strategy, looking for the convenient time and place. We may want to choose the hill to defend; we may want to study our adversary to find the chinks in his armor. We may feel that the cause can best be served by our staying in control, on top of things.

But suppose something entirely different is intended. Suppose the problem is to be solved not so much by our strength or cleverness as by God working in us at that moment.

113

In his prophecy in Mark 13 Jesus says, "And when they bring you to trial and deliver you up, do not be anxious beforehand what you are to say; but say whatever is given you in that hour, for it is not you who speaks, but the Holy Spirit."

To be "mighty" in the biblical sense is to fight with a slingshot, to be ridiculously defenseless. It is to engage the lion bare-handed, to be so simple and foolish.

It is not, of course, to lose one's authenticity as a person, to become characterless. In his worst sufferings Jesus was indestructibly himself

To be "mighty" means to accept the fact that in some situations we have no weapon but naked trust. We do not underestimate the problem or the fierceness of our adversary; we do our homework and pray our prayers. But when the moment of crisis comes and we are about to confront the "thing," whatever the "thing" is, we can only commend ourselves to God.

There is another sort of courage we must not forget: the courage to admit that we are not courageous. We may have to face the fact that the situation or person we are dealing with is too much for us or too much at this moment. Not engaging the lion in the pit is OK so long as we are willing to admit what we are doing or not doing, and in our admission to commend ourselves to God.

Questions for Threes or Fours

1. What situation which needs to be dealt with are you tempted to bypass and why?

2. What resources do you see as available to you in dealing with this situation?

3. Short of dealing with your situation in this head-on way, what other options are open to you?

HOW ARE WE MADE OVER?

Scriptural Content: Acts 8:26-40

The story of the encounter of Philip and the Ethiopian eunuch on the road from Jerusalem to Gaza illustrates for us the problem of the transmission of the gospel: how do you make disciples? Or, put another way, how are people freed to become new in Christ and what role do we play in that *becoming?*

It is clear from our story that there is not *one* way to make disciples. But the story does suggest guidelines. Perhaps a simple listing of them will help:

1. God's redemptive action in Jesus is assumed.

2. So is the desire of the Holy Spirit to transmit the good news of redemption.

3. The means chosen by the Spirit is a chapter from Isaiah —the well known passage about the Suffering Servant from Isaiah 53. This is what the Ethiopian financier sits reading in his comfortable chariot.

4. But he needs an interpreter, someone who can explain the meaning of Isaiah 53 and also the meaning of Jesus.

5. The text tells us that "an angel of the Lord" sent Philip to the Ethiopian. Philip explains the relation of it to the gospel.

6. The effect on the Ethiopian is faith and freedom and immediate baptism and joy.

Application

In reviewing the history of the Christian enterprise, it be-

115

comes clear that our way of making disciples has included all of these steps. We have made sure that the Scriptures are made available to people in a reliable text. We have provided textual criticism, theological interpretation, preaching skills—all the work of our hundreds of well-equipped, brilliantly staffed theological schools. Beyond that we have called and trained witnesses, and we have sent them forth to win and to baptize Christian disciples. We have proclaimed our faith in the work of the Holy Spirit, and we have encouraged our converts to be free and joyful.

But if this is so, why is it that so few people seem to be "new" and to experience that "wow!" of joy which is the gift of the Holy Spirit?

There is certainly no problem with our explanation of the biblical word. It is, without doubt, textually correct and doctrinally sound. Do we not spend millions making sure that our ministers and missionaries are well trained and emotionally healthy?

What then is the difficulty? Could it be in the explainer? Could it be that the explainer of the word which promises to give people newness of life has not himself experienced it? In the early months of 1738 when John Wesley came home after two years as an Anglican missionary in Georgia, he said, "I went to America to convert the heathen, but I found that I myself had not been converted to God." It was only after his heart had been "strangely warmed" in Aldersgate Street, May 24, 1738, that he could write, "I felt I did trust in Christ, Christ alone, for salvation; and an assurance was given me that he had taken away *my* sins, even *mine*, and saved *me* from the law of sin and death."

The emphasis is upon *me, my,* and *mine.* To make disciples is to be personal and relational. Philip climbed into the Ethiopian's chariot, and although we do not know what he said in detail, we may be sure that he talked about the significance of Jesus and his death for him (Philip).

As I have indicated elsewhere in this book, I was myself an explainer and interpreter of the gospel and, I believe, a relatively sincere one. But I was not very personal or relational;

I seem not to have conveyed clearly that I needed Jesus to make me human and personal and to help me build relationships with others. Hence I did not understand what it meant to cry "hallelujah!" At least not very loud. And I didn't set many people free.

Questions for Fours

1. What one person has been the best explainer of the gospel to me and what in his or her explanation was most effective?

2. In explaining the gospel to others what one thing do I need to share which may serve to free them up and to become new beings in Christ?

Alternate Question

After his re-birth or as part of it, the Ethiopian was baptized. Baptism is death and resurrection with our Lord. To what old thing do I need to die, and to what new thing do I need to be committed in the power of the Spirit?

DUMPING THE GARBAGE

Scriptural Content: Matthew 11:28-30

This word of Jesus was probably intended to contrast the burden of the Jewish law with the yoke of Christian discipleship. The heavy ceremonial demands of the Jewish law on the ordinary person, particularly the strict interpretation of these demands by Jesus' contemporaries, aroused our Lord's anger. He saw the relationship between God and man as something much freer and more joyous.

Application

We do not labor under the formal yokes of Judaism or the rigorous demands of earlier forms of Christianity, but we have our assortment of burdens. Perhaps the heaviest load we have to bear is the expectation laid on us in the Western world to be outwardly stoical and cheerful and to hide within us all our unmanageable feelings of anxiety, grief, disappointment, and despair. We are also encouraged to conceal our elations and hilarities. I was recently amused in hearing a young minister reassure his congregation in the face of a visit by some charismatics which might entail such things as glossolalia. It was like a father counselling a child on how to behave when confronted with a seizure.

We must, at all costs, maintain our decorum and not let people know that we are carrying around a load of feelings.

But Jesus encourages us to come to him with what burdens us. And I suspect that what bugs us most of all at this moment is stuff we feel but can't express, broken relationships we cannot heal, circumstances which have gotten beyond our control, or guilt we have no way of dumping. If the TV soap operas are any indication of what America's bread and butter struggles are, the burdens we carry are pretty much that sort of thing.

But what does it mean to come to Jesus with our heavy loads? It certainly means praying to our heavenly Lord and telling him how we truly feel. But it also means finding him where two or three come together in his name (Matthew 18:20).

In several places in the New Testament we are assured that it is God's people who have the keys to the kingdom and the power to bind and loose (Matthew 16:19); the power of effectual agreement (Matthew 18:19); and the right and responsibility to confess and to hear confession (James 5:16). All of this activity is based on the reality of the presence of the risen Christ in the fellowship.

Hence the place to "dump our garbage" is in the supportive fellowship of a few people gathered in Jesus' name. Because Jesus is in the midst of it, such a fellowship cannot only hear us unload but can mediate forgiveness and healing.

One of the greatest surprises of my life came when I dared bring my burden of failure, anxiety, and guilt to two or three gathered in Jesus' name and discovered that I was not put down but forgiven and restored by the fellowship.

Questions for Twos or Threes

1. What particular burden of guilt, sorrow, joy, or hope am I carrying at this moment?

2. How much am I willing to ask of the two or three gathered in Jesus' name in order to ease my yoke and lighten my load?

SMALL EXPECTATIONS

Scriptural Content: Matthew 13:53-58

The story before us concerns a visit of Jesus to his home community; Luke tells of a similar visit (Luke 4:14-30) but places it earlier in Jesus' ministry. In both the Gospels, Jesus' appearance in his hometown generates hostility.

In Matthew the rumor of Jesus' "mighty works" seems to have preceded him; when that is added to the wisdom of his synagogue utterance, the people are both astonished and angry. They deal with these feelings in a very human way. They refuse to believe what they hear. And they justify their attitude by pointing to Jesus, the presumed source of the marvel. They ask, "How can anything so marvelous come from someone so ordinary? Jesus is a carpenter; he is the child of parents we know; he has brothers and sisters whom we know."

Jesus replies with the statement that "a prophet is not without honor except in his own country." What this seems to mean is that to relatives, neighbors, and friends the prophet is too ordinary to have credibility as a worker of miracles. It could also mean that the hometown people refuse, out of envy, to acknowledge what they see coming from him.

In any event, Jesus does not do much in Nazareth. The unbelief of the people blocks them from allowing a climate of wonder and expectancy to develop in them.

Application

Envy paralyzes us so that we cannot see or accept God's work in other people. But unbelief is a worse paralysis. "Isn't this the carpenter's son?" In other words, "What can you expect from him, from them, from it?"

I confess to my shame that for years I asked the same question. I believed in theological not real miracles, I honored a theoretical not a living Spirit. I did not expect to see our sons and our daughters prophesying, our young men seeing visions and our old men dreaming dreams (Acts 2:17). Now this is happening, and I find myself overwhelmed by a tide of wonders which might have been occurring before but without my seeing them.

To me the greatest miracle of all is being sensitized by the Spirit to one another, having that gift of discernment which allows us to see or to sense what is happening to someone we love. A few days ago I passed through some very bruising hours and, as a result, spent a sleepless night. The next morning I had a call from some friends over 500 miles away. They said that during the night they had felt acute anxiety about me and at 3 A.M. had prayed for me. That was the very time I was tossing in bed and unable to sleep. I do not pretend to know what all this means, but I do know that such sensitive love of people for me or my love for them has the quality of wonder.

I feel so enriched by this activity of the Spirit—its fresh surprising character—that I am beginning to understand what Paul writes to the Romans, "How great are God's riches! How deep are his wisdom and knowledge! Who can explain his decisions? Who can understand his ways?" (Romans 11:33 TEV).

Around us lies the desert of our unexpectancy. We see ordinary people leading dull lives; we see threatening minorities, annoyingly impudent young people, unpromising areas of the world; we see the amazing growth of secularism and atheism. We expect nothing and believe nothing.

But then faith is kindled. In the most unexpected places— in an unlikely Nazareth, in a village of Zaire, in a Brazilian ghetto, in an American suburb—a captive is freed, a blind is made to see. Call it a result of the charismatic renewal, established missions, lay witnessing, Faith at Work. The point is that it happens. "It is the Lord's doing, and it is marvelous in our eyes."

Questions for Fours

1. In what unlikely place, circumstance, person, relationship has a miracle happened to me?

2. What place, circumstance, person, relationship seems now to be bound by my small expectation, and what if anything can I do about it?

THE FREEDOM OF FRIENDSHIP

Scriptural Content: Philemon

The letter of Paul to Philemon, though lacking in deep theological content, has something useful to tell us about the dynamics of Christian friendship or brotherliness (sisterliness).

The situation was briefly this. Paul was imprisoned (perhaps in Ephesus). While there he made the acquaintance of Onesimus, a slave of Colossae, and was instrumental in bringing him to faith. It has been assumed that Onesimus was a runaway slave, but the text is not explicit on this point. Whatever the case, Paul has encouraged Onesimus to return to his master and sends this brief letter with him.

John Knox, the eminent New Testament scholar, argues that Paul writes the letter to Philemon not primarily to have Philemon forgive Onesimus and receive him back into his household but in order to have Philemon free Onesimus to return to the prison setting and become helpful to Paul. We may assume that his helpfulness was more than personal. We know that Paul made use of a secretary. In fact this very letter distinguished what Paul writes with his own hand from the rest of the material (v. 19). We also know that Paul employed younger men as his assistants in order to entrust them with carrying on his work. Perhaps he had this in mind for Onesimus.

We don't know. Furthermore, we don't know if Philemon complied with Paul's implied request for Onesimus. What we do know is that in the first decade of the second century, there was an Onesimus who served as bishop of Ephesus and who was helpful to the martyr Ignatius. If this is the slave Onesimus, the action of Paul in writing this letter had wide repercussions in the history of the church.

What is particularly significant in this text is how Paul handles relationships. He begins by affirming Philemon and the friendship, indicating how much it has meant to him.

He continues by asking Philemon to do something for him. If we accept Knox's hypothesis, this something is to free Onesimus for service to Paul. But the Apostle makes this request without manipulating or forcing Philemon. He could have used his apostolic authority, or he could have hooked Philemon by playing on the latter's sympathy. But he does neither. On the other hand, he does not leave either his apostleship or his previous service to Philemon out of the reckoning. In other words, he is not hyper-humble. He is refreshingly human.

What emerges is a triad of people, each one free to be himself and yet each one interdependent. Philemon needs Paul and Onesimus. Paul needs both Philemon and Onesimus. Onesimus needs Philemon and Paul. Each one needs the other but each one stands fast in the freedom with which Christ has made him free.

Application

In reviewing my own friendships I find myself wavering between independence and dependency. Among some people I maintain a kind of uncreative aloofness; with others I go overboard, either asking too much of them or trying to do too much for them. I find myself needing some people so much that I make them dependent on me. Then when they express the needs I have encouraged in them, I feel resentful and am tempted to cop out of the relationship. What I need to work on is the honoring of the other person and myself to the point where I can recognize both the beauty and freedom of personhood and the joy of mutual support.

Questions for Twos

1. With what one person do I now have a free, supportive relationship which allows me to ask for help and to offer

help without playing the role of Lord Bountiful (patronizing) or the role of Obedient Servant (ingratiating)?

2. In what relationship do I find myself most often slipping into a role of generous authority figure ("I'll pick up the tab") or frenzied servant ("Let me do that for you") or overly grateful receiver, ("Oh thank you, kind sir, thank you!") or acutely humble bumbler ("Forgive me, pardon me, excuse me, I didn't mean to")?

3. What further concrete step do I want to take in my friendships which will help me be a loving and beloved friend?

ON BECOMING SOMEONE'S ANANIAS

Scriptural Content: Acts 9:10-19

I have thought much about Ananias, the disciple of Damascus—unfortunate namesake of the Jerusalem Ananias who was a liar. The Lord comes to the Damascus Ananias and says, "Get ready and go to Straight Street and ask for Saul of Tarsus. He is blind and praying. In a vision he has seen you coming to him."

It would be like asking me to go to a house in New York to put my hands on a member of the Mafia or Black Panthers and pray for him.

So Ananias, bless him, says in effect "Wait a minute, Lord, do you know what you are saying? You are asking me to cuddle an asp. This man is the Gestapo and the Mafia rolled into one. In no way will I have anything to do with him."

But the Lord simply restates the request. And Ananias, because of his love for Jesus, goes and puts his hands on the archenemy and calls him "Brother Saul." And from that moment Saul sees again. He is baptized and he eats and his strength is restored.

Application

The beauty of this story lies in the simple salutation, "Brother Saul." The beginning of everything great in the Kingdom of our Lord is this loving identification with other people on the level of their humanity. Out of love God becomes a Gentile to the Gentiles. And here Ananias dares to approach the arrogant enemy of Christians by an act of simple, loving identification- "Brother Saul."

We have sometimes assumed that it takes converted Pharisees to convert Pharisees or Christian academicians to bring other academicians to faith. But what is needed is only loving people looking at other people as human. For it is as human beings and not as experts that we come to faith. Ananias saw a blind, hungry, sleepless, anxious man—the human soul—and blessed and healed him. And for the first time in his life Saul was willing to be nakedly himself, to be Brother Saul, and to accept healing, baptism, nourishment, and love, from the hands of a very ordinary man.

Questions for Fours

1. In the process toward freedom and clearer vision, who has loved me enough to be my Ananias?

2. To whom is the Lord sending me as an Ananias and what are my feelings about going?